information literacy meets Library 2.0

edited by   **Peter Godwin**
and   **Jo Parker**

facet publishing

Published by Facet Publishing, 7 Ridgmount.Street, London WC1E 7AE
www.facetpublishing.co.uk

Facet Publishing is wholly owned by CILIP: the Chartered Institute of Library
and Information Professionals.

British Library Cataloguing in Publication Data
A catalogue record for this book is available from the British Library.

ISBN 978-1-85604-637-4

First published 2008
Reprinted 2009

Typeset from editors' disks in 11/14pt University Old Style and Zurich Expanded
by Facet Publishing.
Printed and made in Great Britain by MPG Books Ltd, Bodmin, Cornwall.

Contents

Contributors

Julie Adams
Julie Adams is manager of the Electronic Information Management Group within Information Services at Staffordshire University. She is responsible for a group of staff who undertake technical web developments for the University and Service websites. Her interests in information literacy include how this can be supported by appropriate technologies and its relationship to IT and other skills. She was a member of the team responsible for developing the CILIP UC & R Award-winning Assignment Survival Kit. She has extensive experience in staff and student IT skills training and is a member of the UCISA-TLIG User Skills Development Working Group.

Laurie Allen
Laurie Allen is the Social Sciences Data Services Librarian at the University of Pennsylvania. As a member of the Research and Instructional Services Department, she is also the liaison to the Urban Studies, Women's Studies, and Criminology Department and bibliographer for Criminology. She also served as chair of the PennTags development team where she brought experience working with students and faculty to the development of the project. She has worked at Penn for five years.

Susan Ariew
Susan Ariew is the Research Services and Collections Librarian for Education at the University of South Florida Tampa Library. She has been a faculty member at the USF Tampa Library since January 2005. Before that time

she worked at Virginia Tech as the College Librarian for Education and Human Development. She spent much of her professional life as an academic librarian, first at the University of Illinois at Urbana-Champaign, at the Center for Research Libraries in Chicago, and then at Virginia Tech. She also taught English, writing, and composition at the high school and collegiate levels for several years.

Marcella Barnhart
Marcella Barnhart is the Assistant Director of the Lippincott Library of the Wharton School, the business library at the University of Pennsylvania. Prior to working at Lippincott she held various training and product development roles at Thomson Scientific. She was a member of the PennTags development team.

Anne-Marie Deitering
Anne-Marie Deitering has been the Undergraduate Services Librarian at Oregon State University since the beginning of 2006. Prior to that, she was the OSU Libraries' Instruction Co-ordinator. At OSU, she serves on the University Assessment Council and the Student Success Council. She speaks and writes frequently about the intersections between student learning, information literacy and the emerging social web.

Christopher Fryer
Christopher Fryer is a systems administrator and web applications developer at the Centre for Learning Technology, London School of Economics. He graduated from University College London with a BSc in Archaeology, and has been working in information technology in higher education since 1999. The LSE Training Portal described in Chapter 8, developed by Chris with Jane Secker, has been shortlisted for an award by the Institute of IT Trainers.

Peter Godwin
Peter Godwin has enjoyed working in various British university libraries including Middlesex, London South Bank and Cambridge. His professional interests have ranged from music and audiovisual materials to information literacy. He draws on many years' experience in academic library management and has presented at conferences in the UK, Europe and USA. He is currently working as an Academic Liaison Librarian at the University of Bedfordshire in Luton.

Cameron Hoffman

Cameron Hoffman is the Information Literacy Librarian at Concordia University Libraries in Montréal, Québec, Canada. He has also worked in an information literacy capacity at the University of Lethbridge. His research work interests involve integrating learning theory into information literacy practice and exploring ways to teach information literacy concepts and skills to distance learners. He is a former English language arts school teacher and has a Masters in Library and Information Studies (MLIS) from the University of Alberta. .

Brian Kelly

Brian Kelly works at UKOLN, a national centre of digital information management, based at the University of Bath. His job title is 'UK Web Focus'. His remit is to advise on emerging new web standards and technologies and on best practices for maximizing the potential of the web. He has been involved in web activities since January 1993 when he helped establish a web service at the University of Leeds – possibly the first institutional university web service in the UK. He has worked at UKOLN since November 1996. His blog is available at http://ukwebfocus.wordpress.com/.

John Kirriemuir

John Kirriemuir, a consultant operating under the name Silversprite (www.silversprite.com), specializes in the use of digital gaming technologies for serious applications in the education, health, business and library sectors. With a research background in digital libraries, and now in his fourth decade as a video game player, he has written over 30 articles and presented in 14 countries on this topic. He lives in the northern periphery of Europe, is learning several Nordic languages, and has long-term research and cultural interests in the social use of internet technologies in this area.

Michelle McLean

Michelle McLean is Information Services Librarian with Casey Cardinia Library Corporation, a public library servicing the outer suburbs of Melbourne (Australia). She is an Associate Member of ALIA, a member of VALA: Libraries and the Future, a regular contributor of book reviews to the *Australian Library Journal* and 2006 recipient of a Ramsay and Reid Scholarship from the State Library of Victoria.

Judy O'Connell

Judy O'Connell is the Head of Library and Information Services at St. Joseph's College, Hunters Hill, NSW, Australia, a leading boarding and day school for boys. Prior to taking up this position in 2008 she was an education consultant for Libraries 2.0 and Web 2.0 for 80 primary and secondary Catholic schools located in the Western region of Sydney, Australia. Her professional leadership experience spans K-12 and tertiary education, with a focus on libraries, technology, curriculum and professional development. She promotes school librarianship at both Australian and international level, and is actively involved with Australian and international school library associations, most recently as Vice President (Associations Relations) of the International Association of School Librarianship. In 2007 she received the John H. Lee Award for innovative use of ICT in learning, jointly awarded by Charles Sturt University and the School Library Association (NSW). Her passion for change and innovation inspires her blog HeyJude which can be found at http://heyjude.wordpress.com.

Jo Parker

Jo Parker manages the Library's Information Literacy Unit at The Open University. Her work ranges from developing learning objects, through to writing courses and experimenting with new technologies. She is a member of the SCONUL Working Group on Information Literacy, and a Fellow of the Higher Education Academy. When not promoting information literacy she can sometimes be found dabbling in Facebook.

Georgina Payne

Georgina Payne has worked at the University of Northampton library since 2002, first working as an e-learning developer and more recently as an Academic Support Manager working with the School of the Arts and the School of Applied Sciences. She is also a module tutor for the University's Business School, lecturing on information management. Before 2002 Georgina worked for the Open University Library developing virtual enquiry services. She is a Chartered librarian and a Fellow of the Higher Education Academy.

Sarah Polkinghorne

Sarah Polkinghorne is a Reference Librarian at the Library of the University of Alberta's Augustana Campus, located in Camrose, Alberta. She reached the world of libraries through the world of the theatre, where she worked as a dramaturg, stage manager, undergraduate instructor and (very infrequent) performer. She now works with faculty across a range of liberal arts and sciences disciplines, designing information literacy instruction for students studying everything from *Oedipus* to econometrics. She considers herself a very fortunate person.

Alison Pope

Alison Pope is a Learning and Teaching Fellow at Staffordshire University, working in Information Services as a Senior Subject and Learning Support Librarian supporting the Schools of Business and Law. Her research interest in information literacy focuses upon the creation of a strategic approach to information literacy with a view to its becoming an embedded and assessed part of the curriculum. Alison has led the Information Literacy Project Working Group at Staffordshire University since 2003 and was a member of the team responsible for developing the CILIP UC & R Award-winning Assignment Survival Kit.

Jane Secker

Jane Secker is Learning Technology Librarian at the Centre for Learning Technology, London School of Economics. She is Chair of the Heron User Group and ALISS (Association of Library and Information professionals in the Social Sciences). She is also the Conference Officer for the CILIP Information Literacy Group and a founder member of LILAC (Librarians' Information Literacy Annual Conference). She has worked on numerous research projects, published widely and has a PhD from the University of Wales, Aberystwyth. The LSE Training Portal described in Chapter 8, developed by Jane with Chris Fryer, has been shortlisted for an award by the Institute of IT Trainers.

Geoff Walton

Geoff Walton is a Subject and Learning Support Librarian at Staffordshire University supporting the Health and Sciences subject areas. He has particular responsibility for Sport and Exercise as well as Psychology. He is also currently a PhD student at Loughborough University where he is researching and developing a new e-learning model for the delivery of information literacy to undergraduate students. He is particularly interested in developing a new e-pedagogy for learning via online social networks. In 2005 he was awarded a Learning and Teaching Fellowship by Staffordshire University in recognition of his excellent contribution to teaching and learning. He is a qualified teacher and a Fellow of the Higher Education Academy.

Sheila Webber

Sheila Webber is Senior Lecturer in the Department of Information Studies, University of Sheffield, where she is Director of the Centre for Information Literacy Research and Director of Learning and Teaching. She is a member of the SCONUL Working Group on Information Literacy. Sheila is frequently invited to speak on information literacy, internet sources and blogging. She maintains the Information Literacy Weblog at http://information-literacy.blogspot.com/ and is Sheila Yoshikawa in Second Life, where she is owner of the Department's Infolit iSchool island.

Jennifer Zimmer

Jennifer Lammers Zimmer is currently Digital Services Librarian at the Kresge Business Administration Library at the Ross School of Business, University of Michigan, Ann Arbor. An avid fan of technology, she takes delight in breaking things while working with Web 2.0 technologies and enjoys the challenge of correcting her mistakes.

Sally Ziph

Sally Ziph is a Senior Associate Librarian at the Kresge Business Administration Library at the Ross School of Business, University of Michigan, Ann Arbor. As Instruction Co-ordinator for a wide range of business students she has come to embrace Web 2.0 formats as indispensable enhancements to classroom instruction.

Acknowledgements

When I first dreamt of producing such a book as this, I was very fortunate to find an ideal co-editor in Jo Parker, whose skills and strengths were to prove so complementary to mine. This has enabled us to work together remarkably painlessly!

This book would have been out of the question without the forbearance of Marcus Woolley and all my long-suffering colleagues at the University of Bedfordshire. It would have been absolutely impossible without the patience and support of my wife, Paula. **Peter Godwin**

I would like to thank Peter for inviting me to be part of such an exciting venture, which enabled me to indulge my editorial tendencies!

I'd also like to thank my colleagues at the OU for their support; apologise to my husband and daughter for my rather brief personal appearances during the production of this book; and point out to my parents that, at last, this is something you can show to people to explain what it is I do! **Jo Parker**

Thanks must go to all our contributors for their willingness to participate, their punctuality and their help in creating this exciting publication.

Every effort has been made to contact the holders of copyright material reproduced in this text, and thanks are due to them for permission to reproduce the material indicated. If there are any queries please contact the publisher.

Peter Godwin and Jo Parker

Part 1
The basics

Chapter 1

Introduction:
making the connections

PETER GODWIN

It's time to stop boring our users with conducted tours of our libraries, earnest library guides, and endless demonstrations of those arcane databases that we love so much. Something has happened. Our users have new mindsets and new expectations. Our information role has spread from buildings and collections to encompass the whole electronic world. Users are creating phenomenal amounts of content individually and collaboratively on the web. We have to recognize the importance of this new landscape in the content we teach. More fundamentally, we now have a new range of tools available to help us transform our teaching into something which is both more fun and more engaging for our users. This is the challenge of Web 2.0 to information literacy (IL). In this introductory chapter we shall investigate why we wrote a book on such a volatile subject, and consider:

- how this affects what we consider to be information literacy
- why we think there is such a phenomenon that can be called Web 2.0
- how this impacts on all sectors of the library world
- case studies which showcase the tools in use and look toward the future.

Why a book?

A book concerning such a movable target as the technologies known as Web 2.0 must be risky. As we enthuse about the exciting new open source tools in perpetual beta available for sharing content on the web, surely it is ironic to do so in a fixed print format? Yet this year there have been a number of excellent guides to Web 2.0 appearing (e.g. Bradley, P. (2007), *How to use Web 2.0 in your Library*, Facet) all in print form. The sheer convenience of print for browsing, review and reference is therefore still demonstrable. We believe that there will be a place for an edited collection of papers to provide you with the background, the definitions, and case studies of those who have blazed the trail in the use of Web 2.0 in relation to information literacy. Our insurance will be a blog to give us the opportunity to add, comment and keep you up to date (*Information Literacy Meets Library 2.0*, at http://infolitlib20.blogspot.com).

Background: a new landscape?

We believe we are living at an exciting turning point in the world of information. It is in this context that we should set the discussions in this book. We shall begin by exploring the information explosion, before discussing the web generation, the Web 2.0 phenomenon and IL.

It is a commonplace to say that we are flooded with information. It was around 2000 that what Thomas Friedman in *The World is Flat* (Friedman, 2006) has called Globalisation 3.0 began and one of the major flatteners in this phenomenon was what he calls 'in-forming'; making knowledge easily available everywhere, to everyone, easily. He continues 'Never before in the history of the planet have so many people – on their own – had the ability to find so much information about so many things and about so many people' (Friedman, 2006, 178). Professors Lyman and Varian at the University of California, Berkeley, have estimated that the world creates as much information each year as the entire Library of Congress print collection 37,000 times over (Albanese, 2006). The assumption that what is required is somewhere on the web is all too familiar a tale to librarians. In the OCLC (2005) report on college students' perceptions of libraries and information resources, 89% went to search engines first for information and only 2% to library websites. The report also concluded that there was a problem about the visibility of library services and materials in the new mass information age. When George M. Needham said 'the librarian as high priest is as dead as Elvis' at the Washington 2007 ALA Conference (Jaschik, 2007), he was suggesting that academic librarians need to look critically at their reference desk practice. As Regalado (2007) says, the library is no longer the prime access point to authoritative information in the age of Google and other search engines. This has caused both consternation and panic among some librarians. However, if we think this over logically, libraries would be totally unable to cope with the millions of questions asked of Google every day. Democratic search is a wonderful thing, and according to Eric Schmidt of Google (quoted in Friedman, 2006, 183), can be 'empowering for humans like nothing else. It is the antithesis of being told or taught . . . about self-empowerment'. In this new world of empowered searchers, librarians need search engines, even though these seem to be answering the kind of questions we think we used to be answering years ago. In response some librarians and library management systems have sought to build federated search engines which can rival freely available search engines, but users habitually begin and end their searches with Google and the like. Massive programmes of digitization by Google and Microsoft may simply exacerbate the problem of information overload (Mann, 2007) without providing adequate means for organizing and mining content. For centuries our users have been information hunters. Now we all have to adapt to the realities of an information-saturated world, in which everyone has unprecedented access to vast quantities of content. It is the cultural response of the generation which has grown up with the web which is becoming so important in driving change.

The 'web generation'

This 'web generation', 'internet generation' or 'Google generation', which dates from 1981, has aroused interest because of its apparent capacity not only to cope with, but also to deal successfully with, the challenges of the modern information environment. Librarians have realized that we have first to become familiar with the study behaviour of this new generation if we are to be relevant to them or engage them (Windham, 2006). The following snapshot seeks to capture the searching behaviour of this generation as experienced by librarians in the USA, and increasingly elsewhere in the world:

- Their use of online information and technology appears natural and effortless.
- They expect single search boxes like Amazon and Google, which give instant satisfaction.

- They need our databases to be in their Virtual Learning Environments (VLEs) or wherever they want to work.
- They find our databases too difficult and have no interest in learning about Boolean logic.
- They like collaboration, team-working and social networking.
- They navigate the web by trial and error, ignoring manuals and helpsheets.
- Their research is self-directed, and likely to be non-linear, for they are hypertext thinkers. This is because they have grown up with PCs and video games.
- Multitasking is a way of life and people live in a state of 'continuous partial attention' (Madden, 2006).
- They think that what is written down and on the web must be correct.
- They work with microcontent: single songs, photos, and blog posts, and are either confused or ignorant about the ethical issues around the content they are using.
- They will cut and paste rather than read and digest what they find.

We must acknowledge that these attributes are stereotypes masking the reality of student bodies which are diverse – full of varying abilities and expectations. These web generation students are not a homogenous group (see Oblinger and Oblinger, 2005, and Kennedy et al., 2006). Some additional indications: the Demos Report (Green and Hannon, 2007) detects a gap between the digital pioneers and most others, and Mitchell (2007) quotes research by I. Hempel which detected significantly more 12- to 26-year-olds as creators, critics and joiners (i.e. Web 2.0 'freaks') than older age groups. This has been described as a divide between 'digital natives' and 'digital immigrants'. Digital natives like to learn using technology: in the EDUCAUSE Center for Applied Research (ECAR) Study (Borreson, Caruso and Salaway, 2007), 72% via internet searches, 53.3% via programmes they can control (e.g. video games), 35.1% via text-based communication, and 32% via blogs, wikis, etc. Recently, a National School Boards Association Report (2007) in the USA demonstrated 96% of students with online access used social networking, and 60% of online students discussed educational topics outside school. This points to the potential for use of these tools in a more formal school situation. Nearly half had uploaded pictures and over 20% had uploaded video. However, their technical knowledge may not be adequate in higher education, and they may lack proficiency in basic academic applications like spreadsheets and statistical packages (Lorenzo et al., 2007). The ECAR Study has been annual and allows longitudinal analysis. From this we learn that participation in social networking leapt from 72.3% in 2006 to 80.3% in 2007. Rating of students' skills using course management systems and presentation software was high and confidence with library online databases considerably lower. We can agree with Head (2007) who concludes: 'Though students clearly had an avid use of MySpace and YouTube, this does not mean college-aged students are natural born researchers.' The reality in 2007 is that their apparent time of search expertise has passed (Regalado, 2007). I have argued elsewhere (Godwin, 2006) that they need encouragement to see across the whole firmament from the Googles, through the gateways, to our hidden databases. The real question is to what extent 'we should move in the direction of the users and how much we should expect users to move in our direction' (McDonald and Thomas, 2006, 6).

Enter Web 2.0

The enthusiasm of the web generation for user content and collaboration compels us to investigate a phenomenon which has been dubbed Web 2.0. This has spawned a whole series of 2.0 subsets, such as Library 2.0, School 2.0, Business 2.0 and so on. But do Web 2.0 and Library 2.0 exist? They have been branded as mere hype (Deschamps, 2007), having reached their peak. By the time you read this, their popularity may even have waned. This does not mean that the activity associated with the Library 2.0 movement will have ended, merely that it may have become mainstream, and be called something else.

What are the characteristics? What makes something 2.0? It's about online applications, interactions and tools which allow individuals to interact, create, and share information using the web as a platform. This can mean that information flows in multiple directions, created and shared by anyone. 'Library 2.0 simply means making your library's space (virtual and physical) more interactive, collaborative, and driven by community needs' (Houghton-John, 2005). This has led to the criticism that this is nothing new, merely what good libraries have always been attempting. The 2.0 world, however, is more volatile in terms of format and function. As we shall see in the analysis by Brian Kelly, in Chapter 2, of the main Web 2.0 tools, there are participatory content systems like blogs and wikis, social sharing services (e.g. del.icio.us, Slideshare), communication tools (social networking sites, such as Facebook), tagging, mashups (combination of two services) and RSS feeds that act as the glue binding the services together. Together with the Google offerings (Scholar and Book Search), they provide a rich new vein of content alongside Wikipedia and the blogosphere. Considerable excitement has been generated by the potential of these tools. But why? Because they offer us a bridge to the web generation and at the same time give us a whole set of new ways to reach our users, and tools with which to teach them.

How should information literacy librarians respond?

We need to be at the forefront of the 2.0 movement in our libraries, championing the content, and trialling the tools to exploit their teaching potential. How does this affect the curriculum for future librarians? Sheila Webber tackles this question in Chapter 3, explaining that Web 2.0's significance in the development of the web will persist and that familiarity with its tools is best achieved by incorporating them into the delivery of courses. Jo Parker also demonstrates this in her later chapter on TU120 Beyond Google, the latest Open University IL course, which both includes how to use Web 2.0 tools and uses them to deliver the IL message of the course. One of the most common outcomes of the clamour around 2.0 has been the growth of training initiatives to help librarians' continuing professional development. The well-known video on YouTube 'The Machine Is Us/ing Us!' (www.youtube.com/watch?v=6gmP4nk0EOE) emphasized the importance of beginning with *us*. We may ask now: has it ended with us? Certainly, in order for librarians to be able to champion the use of these new tools, we have to update and familiarize ourselves first: programmes like Helene Blowers' Learning 2.0: 23 Things, from Charlotte and Mecklenburg County (http://plcmcl2-things.blogspot.com) and Meredith Farkas' Five Weeks to a Social Library (www.sociallibraries.com/course) in the USA have become much re-used, adapted and adopted under Creative Commons licences. So the result may so far be a library workforce that is more 2.0 literate, better able to share and communicate. How has this translated into action? Is it solely up to public librarians or do all librarians need to take note?

Library 2.0 is for everyone

The new read/write web, as it is sometimes called, is affecting all sectors. Educators are debating the need to rethink (again) how they teach in schools at all levels; higher education anticipates a seismic change in student expectations; business is grasping the importance of the new culture for socializing, networking, finding links and marketing; and innovative public libraries are seizing the opportunity to reinvent themselves. This last development is being accelerated by the role of public libraries in providing a level playing field for all ages and backgrounds to access electronic information, prompted by increasingly habitual use of digital communication by commerce and officialdom. Public librarians can provide the facilities for people of all ages to both upskill themselves and become better citizens. In doing so public librarians are experimenting with the use of Web 2.0 tools, such as blogs, MySpace and YouTube. These developments are graphically shown in Michelle McLean's chapter, as she documents her own experience as a public librarian in Australia and in her study trip in the USA in April 2007.

Education in schools in Australia, North America and the UK is being shaken by proponents of the Web 2.0 revolution. Arguments over the pedagogical value of blogging and wikis will continue for a long time, but the enthusiasts grasp that their pupils are developing sophisticated communication and time management skills in their use of technological gadgets and services, which should be linked into educational channels. Sometimes teachers are frustrated by the blocking of sites, and tech-savvy students are frustrated by teachers who are ignorant or even afraid of the online landscape, so 'it's time to revisit, rethink, and revise how technology is implemented in the classroom' (Jones, 2007). Markless (2007) suggests that Web 2.0 has not changed the educational debate and that the same issues keep recurring: the emphasis on inquiry-based learning, active learning and peer collaboration. The new learning environment provides new opportunities to share and re-purpose content. School librarians are also now having to wrestle with these new methods of delivery, and how to support them. Judy O'Connell is our chosen expert to stimulate our interest in the potential for Web 2.0 to connect with pupils in 21st-century schools. The multitasking generation about to enter higher education may be demanding learning that is flexible and multimedia. It is in this sector that we have chosen to concentrate our case studies, which we shall detail later in this chapter.

Much has been written of the use of Web 2.0 in the education sector. But we should not overlook the interest now being shown by business. Special libraries may watch with interest how their employers are debating the merits of the new tools to further their corporate goals, whether internal communication or marketing. It is clear from the Economist Intelligence Unit report (2007) that business is beginning to take Web 2.0 technology seriously. As with academic institutions, progress is often hampered by non-co-operation from IT departments, sheltering behind firewalls, considering it no part of their role to provide support, either fearing or resenting the interference of staff from other departments. Web 2.0 is often about experimentation and losing control. MacManus (2007) refers to two recent Forrester Research reports which tend to show this. Blogwithoutalibrary's survey (Etches-Johnson, 2007), which included corporate, government and law libraries, revealed that 73% of these used RSS, 60% blogs, 46% wikis, 26% instant messaging and 33% social bookmarking. Recently there has been considerable controversy about social networking sites, particularly Facebook, with some firms even banning its use. Tredinnick (2006) sees the possibility of more democratic use of information in organizations, for example, through the use of wikis behind firewalls. This gives librarians here opportunities for experimentation and it suggests that business students need to become familiar with new tools in their studies, in preparation for application both at home and in the office.

From hype to pedagogy

All new fashions are prone to criticism and the 2.0 activity is no exception. That there is nothing new in the central tenets of 2.0 may ring true for user-centred, trend-setting libraries. However it is the juxtaposition of so many of these trends which makes the case for *recognizing* a phenomenon which we can call Library 2.0 more compelling. Much 2.0 activity could be classed as promotional. It has been easy to confuse publicity/promotion with services and particularly instructional material. The need to be where our users are has prompted a lot of discussion and initiatives to push access to them. Should there be links to our databases and catalogue in MySpace or Facebook? Widgets that users can download to their own machine giving easier access to our services are becoming more common, since one of the major reasons that they do not use us can be our lack of visibility. But these are only steps to simpler navigation. As Other Librarian notes, 'it is a fine line between library services and library promotions' (Deschamps, 2007). How many YouTube videos are purely promotional and how many have some element of pedagogy? The advent of TeacherTube may act as a catalyst to improve this. The education TV programme 'Web Literacy' (www.teachers.tv/video/5425), filmed at Wortley School, Leeds, is an excellent example of what can be produced for school use.

How has Web 2.0 affected information literacy?

As the nature of information is changing, so might what it means to be information literate. Kimmo Tuominen (2007) emphasizes the fluidity of the information landscape (blogs, wikis, etc.) and the erosion of context which can cause change in information practices. Certainly the importance of understanding the context of information found will escalate. Tuominen highlights the need to emphasize sociotechnical filtering systems. These can be positive: including automatic ranking by search engines, personal bookmarks and RSS aggregators, and social bookmarking, wikis and participatory news sites; and negative: including blocking software, e-mail blockers, and lists of spoof sites. I do not intend to get into a debate at this point about the overlapping literacies (e.g. ICT, media, electronic, digital). It is more important to acknowledge several obvious developments.

First, taking into account the extra content now available (wikis, blogs, YouTube, podcasts), some students are already questioning why they have to choose from a limited range in their academic work. Why can they not use video, podcasts, and social networks as sources of information? (Mitchell, 2007). We know that students are using Wikipedia and that some academics have difficulties with this, but we are no more able to prevent this than we are their use of Google. Instead we should be telling students using Wikipedia as a starting point how it is constructed. We should encourage their contributions, and view it as collective intelligence, involving judgement and negotiation.

Second, the need for users to be capable of using many of the Web 2.0 tools will become as important as navigating around the keyboard, word-processing or using the web. Surely such use should simply be seen as underpinning individual IL advancement?

Craig Gibson (2007) sees a convergence of prisms (IL, IT fluency and media education) which can assist learners to make connections from information that may seem disparate and to call on a breadth of knowledge to inform decisions. Lorenzo and Dziuban (2006) in their conclusion speak of IL as the possible connector of knowledge which can be taught to young children and continue throughout formal education and life. Joyce Valenza (2007) sees 'two threads – information fluency and Web 2.0 – beautifully woven into rich 21st century cloth as teachers and librarians who value inquiry, thinking skills, ethical behaviour, and innovative work hone their craft on a funky and vibrant 21st century loom, with learners as collaborators'. The new thread of Web 2.0 is dynamic and information literacy is a sturdy fibre. If we accept this underpinning and interweaving, then this can be an exciting time for IL teachers.

I believe that this means that the structure of the major IL frameworks is still valid. This is important for library schools, and Sheila Webber demonstrates in her chapter that, for example, the SCONUL Seven Pillars model is quite capable of accommodating Web 2.0. The only likely effects will be in the detailed application of the models, as, for instance, greater emphasis on evaluation (Pillar 5) and wider application of synthesis leading to new knowledge (Pillar 7).

However, we should focus our attention on one rather ancient and several newer models of IL which may accord more closely with the way that students really search. These are all less linear, more flexible and interesting for the 2.0 world. Williams (2007) draws attention to the berry-picking method of information gathering espoused by Bates (1989), where the user gathers information, not necessarily understanding the exact nature of the subject, using various search methods, following links and gathering information like berries in a bucket. This sounds just like the way many users are using the Web, Google, Wikipedia in the 2.0 world. The Net Lenses model (Edwards, 2006a; 2006b), based on phenomenographic research, presents four approaches to searching (looking for a needle in a haystack; finding your way through a maze; using the tools as a filter; panning for gold) that accord well with web generation behaviours. Hilary Hughes' (2006) model of responses and influences in online information use for learning centres upon a plan-act-record-reflect cycle that users will go through once or several times. Users may jump around the phases, backtrack, or start or finish midway. Synergy here can be detected in the way web generation students operate. Blogging and wikis may be ideal to assist the reflective process that is so important to this model. Beeson (2006) puts the emphasis on the need to inculcate in students 'a critical and reflexive attitude to information, as they read and write it', keeping their search object under review, knowing they 'have to steer through vast seas of information and will have to change course several times on their journey, without losing sight of their overall purpose or interests'.

Using Web 2.0 in the delivery of information literacy

It is in improved delivery of IL that 2.0 offers the greatest challenge. This book is about the early adopters/trend setters from whom other libraries may learn, getting the nuggets they require, ignoring that which doesn't apply. We intend the case studies to showcase the application of the Web 2.0 tools in the teaching of IL. Stemming from higher education in the UK, US or Canada, they reveal a plethora of innovative approaches that demonstrate both engagement with the web generation and pedagogical value.

Blogs are often cited as powerful agents for reflecting on the individual learning experience (Windham, 2007). We have included a carefully organized experiment at the University of Northampton, 'Enrage or engage: the blog as an assessment tool' by Georgina Payne, in which a blog assessment is used with first-year business school students.

Wikis help users to understand how information, and hence perhaps knowledge, is formed, by using the content creation functions in Wikipedia. We learn from experiments at Oregon State University how Wikipedia can be used creatively to foster understanding of how to use material to form a researched argument, in Anne-Marie Deitering's case study 'Using Wikipedia to eavesdrop on the scholarly conversation'.

RSS (Really Simple Syndication) enables us to make full use of social software in libraries. Jane Secker and Christopher Fryer of the London School of Economics and Political Science tell us how they use RSS to enhance their training outreach in their case study 'Information Literacy and RSS feeds at LSE'.

Podcasts seemed a logical development to follow existing web-based teaching methods at Kresge Business Administration Library, Michigan. Jennifer Zimmer and Sally Ziph in 'Library instruction on the go: podcasting at the Kresge Library' tell the story of their evolving podcasting and vodcasting services.

The potential of user tagging was spotted early at University of Pennsylvania, and Laurie Allen and Marcella Barnhart describe how this was used in PennTags, their social bookmarking tool.

Flickr is one of the most popular photo-sharing services currently on the web. The tagging facility can be used to help students appreciate the value of subject searching and understand the differences between natural and controlled vocabularies. Sarah Polkinghorne, University of Alberta, and Cameron Hoffman, Concordia University Libraries, provide a stimulating case study 'Sparking Flickrs of insight into controlled vocabularies and subject searching'.

YouTube can prove to be a useful resource for locating IL material and Susan Ariew, University of South Florida, explains how her library has employed it to host the instructional videos developed there in 'Joining the YouTube conversation to teach information literacy'.

In 2006, when the Open University reviewed its first IL course, U120 MOSAIC, it decided that a rewrite was necessary which would introduce Web 2.0 tools to students and also employ them in the delivery of the course. Jo Parker guides us through the process by which this revamped course has become Web 2.0 compliant in 'Going beyond Google at the Open University'.

Libraries that produce web-based instructional material are always looking at alternative ways to present it. The Assignment Survival Kit (ASK) at Staffordshire University is a good example of this. Alison Pope and colleagues run through the genesis and development of this guide in the case study 'Using Web 2.0 to enhance the Staffordshire University Assignment Survival Kit'.

What else may be Web 2.0?

Is gaming Library 2.0? Its growing use in libraries has led it to be grouped alongside the usual 2.0 tools and we have decided to include a discussion of it here. There are obvious parallels in its promotion of active learning and usefulness for engaging the web generation. John Kirriemuir, in his chapter entitled 'Teaching information literacy through digital games', provides a concise introduction to the use of gaming in libraries and some major projects which involve IL delivery.

Second Life teased us at first: was it a game or something else? Despite being able to mash favourite Web 2.0 tools into Second Life (Cashmore, 2006) we did not see it as essentially Web 2.0 when we set out. We have therefore chosen to keep more in-depth discussion of it until the Conclusion.

What we are learning

Web 2.0 has struck a vital chord with librarians and the enthusiasm which has led to Library 2.0 has again shown how librarians are prepared to be forward looking and to help drive change both institutionally and within society. Both the sectoral chapters and case studies generate a feeling of great excitement and demonstrate a 'can-do' mentality. This may spring from the use of the web as a platform and open source software, which is not dependent on support from IT departments, thus setting librarians free to experiment and develop their good ideas. Costs are usually low, except for staff time, but sustainability of these open source applications carries the risk of replacement by new technologies as they arise. The Web 2.0 mantra allows users to be involved in the continuous process of change, providing feedback and critical evaluation. These bottom-up approaches could inspire and encourage library staff everywhere, but are we ready for them?

References

Albanese, A. R. (2006) Google is not the Net, *Library Journal*,
www.libraryjournal.com/article/CA6370224.html.

Bates, M. J. (1989) *The Design of Browsing and Berry-picking Techniques for the Online Search Interface*,
www.gseis.ucla.edu/faculty/bates/berrypicking.html.

Beeson, I. (2006) Judging Relevance: a problem for e-literacy, *Italics,* **5** (4),
www.ics.heacademy.ac.uk/italics/vol5iss4/beeson.pdf.

Borreson Caruso, J. and Salaway, G. (2007) *The ECAR Study of Undergraduate Students and Information Technology,* EDUCAUSE Center for Applied Research, www.educause.edu/ir/library/pdf/ers0706/ekf0706.pdf.

Cashmore, P. (2006) SecondLife + Web 2.0 = Virtual World mashups, *Mashable Socialnetworking News,* http://mashable.com/2006/05/30/second-life-web-20-virtual-world-mashups.

Deschamps, R. (2007) We Asked for Web 2.0 Libraries and We Got 2.0 Librarians, *The Other Librarian* (blog),
http://otherlibrarian.wordpress.com/2007/08/15/we-asked-for-20-libraries-and-we-got-20-librarians.

Economist Intelligence Unit (2007) Serious Business; Web 2.0 goes corporate, http://graphics.eiu.com/upload/eb/fast_report.pdf.

Edwards, S. L. (2006a) *Introducing the Net Lenses Model: an electronic outcome space*, www.edu.hku.hk/earli/Sylvia%20Lauretta%20Edwards.doc.

Edwards, S. L. (2006b) *Net Lenses: searching explained*,
    www.netlenses.fit.qut.edu.au/searching.

Etches-Johnson, A. (2007) A Long-overdue Update on the Special Library 2.0
    Survey, *Blogwithoutalibrary* (blog),
    www.blogwithoutalibrary.net/?m=200701.

Friedman, T. L. (2006) *The World is Flat: the globalized world in the twenty-first
    century*, Penguin.

Gibson, C. (2007) *Prisms Around Student Learning: information literacy, IT
    fluency, and media literacy*, www.educause.edu/ir/library/pdf/ELI07302.pdf.

Godwin, P. (2006) Keeping Up With the Google Generation. In Walton, G. and
    Pope, A. (eds), *Information Literacy: recognising the need*, Chandos.

Green, H. and Hannon, C. (2007) *Their Space: education for a digital generation*,
    www.demos.co.uk/publications/theirspace, Demos.

Head, A. J. (2007) Beyond Google: how do students conduct academic
    research?, *First Monday*, **12** (8),
    www.firstmonday.org/issues/issue12_8/head.

Houghton-John, S. (2005) Library 2.0 Discussion: Michael squared,
    LibrarianinBlack (blog),
    http://librarianinblack.typepad.com/librarianinblack/2005/12/
    library_20_disc.html.

Hughes, H. (2006) Responses and Influences: a model of online information
    use for learning, *Information Research*, **12** (1), Paper 279,
    http://informationr.net/ir/12-1/paper279.html.

Jaschik, S. (2007) When 'Digital Natives' Go to the Library, *Inside Higher
    Education*, www.insidehighered.com/news/2007/06/25/games.

Jones, K. (2007) *Digital Literacy in a 2.0 World*,
    www.slideshare.net/thecorkboard/digital-literacy-in-a-20-world.

Kennedy G., Krause, K., Judd, T., Churchward, A. and Gray, K. (2006) *First Year
    Students' Experiences with Technology: are they really digital natives?*,
    www.bmu.unimelb.edu.au/research/munatives/natives_report2006.pdf.

Lorenzo, G. and Dziuban, C. (2006) *Ensuring the Net Generation is Net Savvy*,
    ELI Paper 2, www.educause.edu/ir/library/pdf/ELI3006.pdf.

Lorenzo, G., Oblinger, D. and Dziuban, C. (2007) How Choice, Co-creation,
    and Culture are Changing What it Means to be Net Savvy, *Educause
    Quarterly*, **30** (1), 6–12.

MacManus, R. (2007) Fear of Web 2.0, *Read/WriteWeb* (blog),
    www.readwriteweb.com/archives/fear_of_web_20.php.

Madden, M. (2006) *Young and Wired: how today's young tech elite will influence the libraries of tomorrow*. Presented at Tampa Bay Library Consortium Annual Meeting, 11 March 2006, www.slideshare.net/hoganedix/young-and-wired-the-pew-foundation.

Mann, T. (2007) *The Peloponnesian War and the Future of Reference, Cataloguing, and Scholarship in Research Libraries,* http://guild2910.org/Pelopponesian%20War%20June%2013%202007.pdf.

Markless, S. (2007) *Information Literacy and the Future of Learning,* www.slideshare.net/SLA/information-literacy-and-the-future-of-learning.

McDonald, R. H. and Thomas, C. (2006) Disconnects Between Library Culture and Millennial Generation Values, *Educause Quarterly,* **29** (4).

Mitchell, P. (2007) *Information Literacy Experts or Expats?* SLANZA Conference, School Library of New Zealand Aotearoa Conference, Wellington, 2007, www.educationau.edu.au/jahia/webdav/site/myjahiasite/shared/papers/slanza_pm.pdf.

National School Boards Association (2007) *Creating & Connecting: research and guidelines on online social – and educational – networking,* www.nsba.org/site/pdf.asp?TP=/site/docs/41400/41340.pdf.

Oblinger, D. G. and Oblinger, J. L. (2005) Is it Age or IT: first steps toward understanding the Net Generation. In Oblinger, D. G. and Oblinger, J. L. (eds), *Educating the Net Generation,* www.educause.edu/ir/library/pdf/pub7101.pdf.

OCLC (2005) *Perceptions of Libraries and Information Resources,* www.oclc.org/reports/2005perceptions.htm.

Regalado, M. (2007) Research Authority in the Age of Google, *Library Philosophy and Practice,* Special issue, www.webpages.uidaho.edu/~mbolin/regalado.pdf.

Tredinnick, L. (2006) Web 2.0 and Business, *Business Information Review,* **23** (4), 228–34.

Tuominen, K. (2007) *Information Literacy 2.0.* Keynote address at Making a Difference: moving toward Library 2.0 conference, Helsinki, 7 May 2007, http://lib.eduskunta.fi/dman/Document.phx/Julkaisut/Puheet%20ja%20esitykset/Information%20Literacy?folderId=Julkaisut%2FPuheet%2Bja%2Besitykset&cmd=download.

Valenza, J. K. (2007) *Web 2.0 Meets Information Literacy,* IFLA SL Newsletter (blog), http://iflaslblog.wordpress.com/2007/07/02/web-20-meets-information-literacy.

Williams, G. (2007) Unclear on the Context: refocusing on information
    literacy's evaluative component in the age of Google, *Library Philosophy and
    Practice*, Special issue, www.webpages.uidaho.edu/~mbolin/williams.htm.
Windham, C. (2006) Getting Past Google: perspectives on information literacy
    from the millennial mind, ELI Paper 3,
    www.educause.edu/ir/library/pdf/ELI3007.pdf.
Windham, C. (2007) Reflecting, Writing, and Responding: reasons students
    blog, ELI Paper 2,
    http://connect.educause.edu/library/abstract/ReflectingWritingand/39344.

Chapter 2

Library 2.0 and information literacy: the tools

BRIAN KELLY

Introduction

When the world wide web (the web) first became popular in the mid-1990s its move beyond its roots in academia helped transform people's expectations of the services which IT could provide. Initially large firms, at first those in the IT business but then across many other sectors, began to provide information services about their activities. Then, as the cost of network bandwidth became cheaper and broadband access became widely available, smaller organizations, and individuals, began to provide a presence on the web.

This initial use of the web tended to focus on the provision of static information resources. The provision of these services would typically be managed by a centralized team within the organization which would be responsible for ensuring that publications on the website complied with legal requirements and organizational guidelines. The team would make sure that the information reflected the official views of the organization, and complied with guidelines covering content, the appearance of the resources and various technological requirements.

We are now seeing a radical change in the ways in which the web is used. Rather than simply providing information the web is being used as a communications and collaboration tool. These changes will require new approaches to web management in order to take advantage of the new opportunities that are becoming available.

The changes in patterns of web usage have resulted in the coining of the term 'Web 2.0' to enable us to talk about these two distinct approaches. This chapter explains in more detail the main characteristics of Web 2.0 and provides an introduction to a variety of Web 2.0 application areas. The chapter discusses a variety of tools including blogs, wikis, syndication formats (such as RSS - Really Simple Syndication), communications technologies (such as instant messaging and Skype), social networking and social bookmarking applications, podcasts and videocasts, tagging and folksonomies, mashups and virtual worlds. The chapter concludes by providing examples of how you can make use of these tools.

Web 2.0 concepts

The term 'Web 2.0' was coined by Tim O'Reilly (2005) to describe an emerging pattern of new uses of the web and approaches to web development, rather than a formal upgrade of web technologies as the 2.0 version number may appear to signify.

The key Web 2.0 concepts include:

- *It's an attitude, not a technology*: an open acknowledgement that a key aspect of Web 2.0 is not about a set of technical standards or applications, but a new mindset to how the web can be used.
- *The network effect*: this describes services which become more effective as the number of users increases. This effect is well known in computer networks, with the internet providing a good example of how internet traffic can be more resilient as the number of devices on the internet grows. The network effect also applies to business models and the ways in which technologies can become more ubiquitous: for example, at one extreme, a telephone is useless when there is only one user, but its potential benefits grow as the number of users increases. In an environment in which large sectors of society have access to a mobile phone for most of their waking hours, we are seeing how this can transform social contacts (e.g. regular text messaging) and provide more flexibility than was possible in the past.
- *Openness*: the development of more liberal licences (copyright licences such as Creative Commons; open source licences for software) can allow integration of data and re-use of software without encountering legal barriers.
- *The long tail*: as more people use the web, business opportunities

emerge for niche markets which previously it may not have been cost-effective to reach. Wikipedia defines the effect of the long tail as follows: 'Businesses with distribution power can sell a greater volume of otherwise hard to find items at small volumes than of popular items at large volumes' (http://en.wikipedia.org/wiki/The_Long_Tail).

- *Trust your users*: the openness described above can also include a willingness to engage more openly with service users and active engagement in discussions, debate and sharing of resources. This approach to openness should be a feature of public sector and educational organizations. In addition the potential benefits of greater openness within the commercial sector have given rise to the term 'radical trust' which encapsulates its meaning in the phrase 'The age of persuasion is over, welcome to the age of dialogue' (Radical Trust, 2006). The long tail can have particular benefits within the educational and library sectors, which often have a requirement to support the needs of minority groups or niche interests.

- *Network as a platform*: the web can now be used to provide access to web applications, and not just information resources. This allows users to make use of applications without having to go through the cumbersome exercise of installing software on their local PC.

- *Always beta*: with web applications being managed on a small number of central servers rather than on a large number of desktop computers, it becomes possible for the applications to be enhanced in an incremental fashion, with no requirement for users of the application to upgrade their system.

- *Small pieces, loosely coupled*: as the technical infrastructure of the web stabilizes, it becomes possible to integrate small applications. This enables services to be developed more rapidly and can avoid the difficulties of developing and maintaining more complex and cumbersome systems.

A useful summary of Web 2.0, which includes details of criticisms raised concerning the Web 2.0 term, is provided in Wikipedia (http://en.wikipedia.org/wiki/Web_2).

Web 2.0 tools

The summary given above illustrates some of the key concepts which are embedded in many of the Web 2.0 application areas. But what are the key application areas which embody the Web 2.0 concepts? The most popular application areas associated with Web 2.0 include:

- *Blogs*: applications which are commonly used to provide diaries, with entries provided in chronological order. There are now many diverse ways in which blogs can be used.
- *Wikis*: collaborative web-based authoring tools. The best-known example of a wiki is Wikipedia, a global encyclopedia which was developed through the collaborative effort of many volunteers around the world.
- *Syndicated content*: technologies which allow content to be automatically embedded elsewhere.
- *Podcasts and videocasts*: syndicated audio and video content, which is often transferred automatically to portable MP3 players such as iPods.
- *Mashups*: services which contain data and services from multiple sources. A mashup often incorporates syndicated content, although there are other ways of creating mashups.
- *Social sharing services*: applications which provide sharing of various types of resources such as bookmarks, photographs, etc.
- *Communications tools*: various tools including chat applications (such as MSN Messenger) and internet telephony tools (such as Skype) which can provide various forms of communication ranging from simple text messaging systems through to audio and video communications.
- *Social networks*: communal spaces which can be used for group discussions and sharing of resources.
- *Folksonomies and tagging*: a bottom-up approach to providing descriptive labels for resources, to allow them to be retrieved.
- *Virtual worlds*: 3D simulations in which avatars (which represent the user) can interact with other users.

A better appreciation of these concepts can be gained by looking at some specific examples in more detail.

Blogs

A blog is a website in which the entries are written in chronological order and displayed with the most recent entries at the top. In this respect they have many parallels with personal diaries and they are often used in this way, both for personal and professional purposes, with use by learners to reflect on their learning illustrating the hybrid aspects of blogs and other Web 2.0 technologies.

The key aspects of blogs that make them appealing for use in a library context include the ease of creation of content (typically using a web-based authoring environment which is part of the blog service), simple use of categories (which allows related blog postings to be accessed), a stable address (known as a 'permalink') which allows individual blog postings to be referred to, a 'ping-back' mechanism that notifies authors when other blogs have cited their posts and the ability to allow users to give their comments on blog posts.

Although many blogging software applications can be downloaded and installed on a local server, there are also many externally hosted services, such as Blogger (www.blogger.com) and WordPress (www.wordpress.com), which enable blogs to be deployed without the need to install software locally.

The provision of services by third-party companies is a common feature in many Web 2.0 application areas and has helped in the take-up of such services, especially within organizations with limited technical expertise. It should be pointed out, though, that the use of externally hosted services does have some risks, especially regarding the long- term sustainability of the services. Before making any decision to adopt this approach it would be advisable to carry out a risk assessment, which might include finding out more about the company that provides the service and the length of time the service has been available. It would also be advisable to ensure that it would be possible to export any data you have created using the service and re-import it into an alternative service.

Wikis

A wiki refers to a collaborative web-based authoring environment. The term wiki comes from a Hawaiian word meaning 'quick' and the origins of the name reflect the aims of the original design of wikis to provide a very simple authoring environment that allows web content to be created without the need to learn the HTML language or to install and master HTML authoring tools. To create or edit content in a wiki one simply needs to click on the edit option within a wiki web page and then use a very simple mark-up language or simple editing interface to create a simple structure for the page (headings, lists and embedded images, for example).

The best-known example of a wiki is probably Wikipedia (www.wikipedia com) which provides a global encyclopedia of content provided by volunteers worldwide. Wikipedia's popularity provides an example of both the ease of use which wiki software can provide and the Web 2.0 philosophy of trusting your users. It should be noted, though, that Wikipedia is just one example of a wiki service, in this case based on use of the MediaWiki software (www.mediawiki.org). There is a wide range of wiki software tools available and many different ways in which wikis are being used.

Syndicated content

Blogs and wikis can make it easy to create web content. However, an even simpler way of providing content is to use content which is syndicated by others. Technologies such as RSS (which now usually refers to Really Simple Syndication) and Atom allow content provided in a simple XML format to be automatically transferred and converted into HTML for display in a web page or used in other applications.

Blog applications were the first to popularize the concept of syndicated content using the RSS standard. The majority of blogging applications provide RSS feeds of blog posts, allowing the content to be easily embedded elsewhere. A popular use of RSS feeds is for reading multiple blogs: rather than having to go to multiple blog websites, the RSS feed for each blog can be added to an RSS reader, which can be a web-based blog reader such as Bloglines (www.bloglines.com) or Google Reader (www.google.com/reader/view) or a dedicated desktop application such as Blogbridge (www.blogbridge.com).

The popularity of RSS in enabling content from blogs to be re-used in a variety of other applications led to RSS being used much more widely. Initially RSS was regarded as a news feed syndication, with websites providing news about their services (typically on their home page) and the content being provided as an RSS feed which could be re-used elsewhere. The ease of use and other benefits of this approach then led to RSS being used as a general mechanism both for providing alerts of changes and for syndicating content. RSS feeds can be used, for example, for providing news about new publications available in the library and details about forthcoming events, as well as allowing content to be replicated to other environments, such as a list of publications to be embedded across a range of websites.

Podcasts and videocasts

Syndication technologies can be used not just for text and images, but also for audio and video files. The term 'podcast' was coined to describe a development to the RSS standard that enabled binary files, such as MP3 audio files, to be syndicated. In this case, rather than syndicating a resource to another website, the resource could be transferred to a PC and then synchronized with a portable MP3 player such as an iPod. As MP3 players became more sophisticated, this concept was extended to enable the syndication of video files. Podcasts have a particular benefit in enabling people to listen to audio resources while travelling. It remains to be seen, though, whether videocasts will take off in this way, as the small size of the screen on mobile devices adversely affects the quality of the experience in a way that is not applicable to audio.

Mashups

A mashup is a web service which combines data or services from more than one source. A popular form of mashup makes use of Google Maps to provide location data (e.g. location of library services). In the case of Google Maps, the service can be embedded within a website through use of JavaScript, but other technologies can also be used. Syndicated content provided by RSS is also often embedded in a mashup application.

The term 'mashup' originates in music and is used to describe music which is integrated from a number of sources. The meaning can also be applied to mashups used in web applications such as the 'Ray of Light' video (2003) available on YouTube (www.youtube.com) which was produced at St Joseph's Public Library. The promotional video for the library service shows a speeded-up day in the life of staff at the library and uses Madonna's 'Ray of Light' song as backing music.

It should be noted that there are likely to be legal implications in the production of mashup services. However, as has been seen in an agreement reached between Google (owners of the YouTube service) and Warner Music Group (TechCrunch, 2006) content owners may see new marketing opportunities and business models opening up and may be willing to change their policies on re-use of content. The decision would appear to have legitimized the use of Madonna's music in the 'Ray of Light' video described above.

Social sharing services

We have seen a number of application areas that make it easier for users to create content and enable that content to be re-used more easily. Social sharing services build on the ease of use provided by blog and wiki technologies and focus on the benefits of collaboration.

As an example, consider how bookmarking services have developed. Many users will have used the bookmarking tools available in their web browser. Web browsers, including Internet Explorer, Firefox and Opera, provide bookmarking capabilities that allow the addresses of web pages to be noted so that they can easily be revisited.

Social bookmarking services build on this concept but allow the address of the web resource to be stored remotely and shared with others. This provides a number of advantages to the user. For example, the resources can be accessed from any computer, not just the one which is normally used, but more important is the network effect that the collaborative sharing of bookmarks can provide.

An example of the collaborative aspects of using a shared bookmarking service can be seen from the screen image of the del.icio.us service (http://del.icio.us) shown in Figure 2.1. This page was used to bookmark resources used in a talk on Web 2.0 at the CILIP (Chartered Institute of Library and Information Professionals) Career Development Group's annual conference. Making use of a public bookmarking service allows the conference participants (and others) to access the resources mentioned after the event. And, in addition, it is possible to see not only the resources the creator has bookmarked but also details of other del.icio.us users who have bookmarked these resources. As can be seen in the diagram, 46 del.icio.us users bookmarked the UK Web Focus blog. This allows access to other resources bookmarked by these users, which can help to find related resources.

The advantages of sharing bookmarks also apply to sharing other types of resources, such as photographs, videos, PowerPoint presentations, and so on. The Flickr service (www.flickr.com) is one of the best known photographic sharing services, with YouTube (www.youtube.com) and Google Video (http://video.google.co.uk) both very popular for sharing videos.

The SlideShare service (www.slideshare.com) provides an example of a Web 2.0 service which can be used to share presentations created in Microsoft PowerPoint or other presentation tools. Once a presentation is uploaded to the service it can be viewed on the SlideShare website,

Figure 2.1   Example of the del.icio.us social bookmarking service (taken from http://del.icio.us/lisbk/cilip-cdg-2007-04)

Reproduced with thanks by permission of Yahoo! Inc.® 2007 by Yahoo! Inc. YAHOO! and the YAHOO! logo are trademarks of Yahoo! Inc.

embedded in blogs or other websites or the file downloaded for use locally. As can be seen in Figure 2.2 on page 28, Slideshare enables users to provide comments on the presentation and also to bookmark the resource (in this case, by adding it to their list of favourites). Again, as with del.icio.us, it is possible to view related presentations, including others uploaded by the same user or presentations they have added to lists of favourite presentations.

Communications tools

Wikis support collaborative working by providing mechanisms for joint creation and maintenance of content, while blogs can not only be used by teams as well as individuals but also allow users to provide feedback on the contents of blog postings.

Communications tools can complement these collaborative tools by enabling direct communication between two or more individuals. Instant Messaging (IM) tools provide more immediacy than e-mail, and often avoid the annoyance of spam, which is turning many users away from e-mail. Popular instant messaging applications, such as MSN Messenger and

Figure 2.2 The SlideShare service (taken from
www.slideshare.net/lisbk/introduction-to-facebook-
opportunities-and-challenges-for-the-institution)
Reproduced with thanks.

Yahoo! Messenger, now provide much more functionality than just allowing small groups to send short messages to each other, and these services can also provide audio and video communications. More effective use of audio can be provided using dedicated VoIP (Voice over IP) applications, the best known of which is probably Skype.

The current generation of communications tools provides text, audio and video capabilities and state of presence (to allow you to see if your colleagues are online). They may also be extensible (allowing additional functionality, such as collaborative web browsing, to be added to the application) or have the ability to be embedded in web pages. An example of embedding a communications tool with a web page can be seen on the University of Teesside Library website (http://lis.tees.ac.uk/chat) which provides access to the Meebo application (www.meebo.com) for live communications with a staff member in the Library.

Social networks
Social networking services, such as Bebo (www.bebo.com), MySpace

(www.myspace.com) and Facebook (www.facebook.com), provide an integrated environment that allows users to share resources, discuss their shared interests and discover others with similar interests. Social networks have proved very popular with young people, with services such as MySpace providing an environment which is widely used for informal chats and discussions of shared interests, such as music. More recently there has been a significant growth in usage of Facebook, especially in the education sector, with many students in universities, colleges and schools making regular use of the service.

The take-up of social networking services such as Facebook has prompted educational institutions and libraries to explore their potential in supporting institutional aims. Universities, for example, may wish to browse public message archives to find out more about what their user communities are saying about their services and any areas of concern that are being discussed. A further development may be to provide access to institutional services from *within* social networking services. This can range from providing access to institutional RSS feeds (e.g. news about library services) through to access to the search interfaces of library databases.

Facebook is currently the focus of much discussion on the role it can provide, not only to support informal learning and access to institutional information, but also as a forum for discussions by library staff. A Facebook group on Librarians and Facebook (http://bathac.facebook.com/group. php?/gid=2210901334) has attracted over 2000 members who are interested in discussing the potential of Facebook in supporting the aims of the library sector.

Folksonomies and tagging

A challenge for users of many Web 2.0 services is finding relevant resources. The approach developed that builds on the ease of use in the creation of content is known as tagging. This allows the content creator to provide simple search terms (tags) that can be used for finding resources. The term 'folksonomy' has been coined to describe this bottom-up approach to the provision of metadata. This contrasts with the traditional approach which requires skilled cataloguers to assign appropriate keywords from well established lists of controlled vocabularies. Many Web 2.0 services provide interfaces which allow the content creator to define their preferred tags for a resource, as we have seen previously in the cases of del.icio.us and

SlideShare. Having found a particular resource, the tag provides links to other resources with the same tag. Although this approach to the provision of metadata for resource discovery has clear limitations (tags which have alternative meanings, lack of quality control, etc.), in practice it affords an ease of use that formal approaches to cataloguing may lack. This is ideal for general users who do not have specialist information retrieval skills.

Uses of this approach have been illustrated in the examples of the del.icio.us and SlideShare services. In addition to browsing for tags within a particular service, tags can be indexed by search engines, just as Google indexes the content of web pages. The Technorati search engine (www. technorati.com) provides a search engine for tags provided on a variety of Web 2.0 services, including blogs, Flickr and YouTube.

Virtual worlds

Second Life is probably the best-known example of a virtual world – a computer-based simulation of an environment in which users interact using 3D models known as avatars. Although initially developed as an environment for testing 3D computer games, Second Life is not itself a game, but rather provides a virtual world that can be used for a wide variety of purposes.

There is growing interest in the use of Second Life in particular within the educational and cultural heritage sectors, with examples of university buildings, libraries and museums now being found in Second Life – see Figure 2.3. We are currently seeing experimentation into the potential of virtual worlds to provide enriched learning experiences, simulations of alternative realities and 3D models of real world environments.

Using the tools
Accessing Web 2.0 as a reader
Using Technorati

The Web 2.0 applications described here can be accessed using modern web browsers, including Internet Explorer, Firefox and Opera. A good way of beginning to appreciate the potential benefits that use of Web 2.0 provides is to use the various tools to support your information needs. One approach might be to use various tools and services to find information about your organization or an area of interest.

The Technorati search engine provides an index of RSS feeds from various Web 2.0 applications such as blogs, YouTube, etc. Whereas Google

Figure 2.3   A library in Second Life (http://secondlife.com)
Reproduced with thanks.

provides a valuable search engine for finding authoritative sources of information, Technorati complements Google by finding recent sources of information on a topic. Technorati can therefore be a valuable tool for the information professional. Use of Technorati can be made even easier if the Technorati search engine plugin is added to the standard search box provided in Firefox, as this means that you will not have to go to the Technorati website to make use of it. (Technorati can also be added to the Internet Explorer browser's search facility, although it is slightly more tricky to do this.)

Using del.icio.us

If you wish to be able to easily revisit a useful web resource, perhaps one you found using Technorati, you may find it useful to set up an account on a social bookmarking service such as del.icio.us. Use of services such as del.icio.us can be made much easier if you add the service's bookmarking tool to your browser. This can be done by simply dragging an icon on the service's web page onto your browser toolbar.

Once you have registered for an account and added the bookmarking tool to your browser, click on the icon when you are visiting a page that you wish to add to your collection of shared bookmarks. You will then need to add an appropriate tag and can optionally include a brief description of the page.

Using a Web 2.0 repository

If you are involved in user training or staff development you will find that a wide range of training materials on the use of Web 2.0 technologies is available via various Web 2.0 services. The SlideShare repository of presentations can be a useful starting point if you are looking for a slideshow which you can download, adapt and use. You should find that many of the slideshows are provided with a Creative Commons licence which will allow you to reuse the materials, but if this is not the case you can still use the materials as a self-study resource.

Many multimedia training and educational resources about Web 2.0 are available on services such as YouTube and Google Video or as podcasts. The resources may be used in training courses or for individual learning. An alternative approach would be to make use of podcast resources. This may be particularly useful for those who have long journeys to work, as the learning can take place while travelling.

Using Netvibes or Pageflakes

The Technorati and del.icio.us services, like many Web 2.0 services, provide RSS feeds of the information they hold. Rather than having to go to each of these services on a regular basis you may find it easier to bring together the information into a single place using an RSS aggregation service. Two popular web-based RSS aggregators are Netvibes (www.netvibes.com) and Pageflakes (www.pageflakes.com). Once you have subscribed to one of these free services you can add your RSS feeds, which will provide a unified view of your resources. More importantly, you can also use the service to include content which is changing, such as blogs that you may be interested in reading. Many Web 2.0 services also provide an RSS feed for dynamically changing content. An example of this is Technorati, which can provide an RSS feed associated with a particular tag.

Figure 2.4 illustrates a page on Pageflakes which displays the RSS feeds for:

- in the left hand column, the UKOLN news feeds and the UK Web Focus blog,
- in the middle column, alerts for new Technorati search results for posts containing 'UKOLN' and recent changes to a Wetpaint wiki used to support an event on 'Sharing Made Simple'
- in the right hand column, a Google alert for search results for the term 'UKOLN' and for a set of del.icio.us bookmarks.

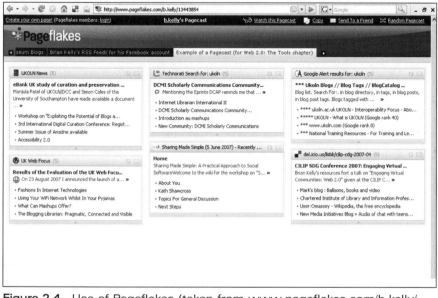

Figure 2.4   Use of Pageflakes (taken from www.pageflakes.com/b.kelly/13443854)

Reproduced with thanks by permission of Pageflakes Inc.

Accessing Web 2.0 as a creator
Using a blog

We have seen how easy it is to exploit the benefits of Web 2.0 services in order to discover and manage access to interesting resources. If you wish to be a content creator in a Web 2.0 environment this may require a greater level of commitment, although this need not necessarily be the case, because as we have seen, simply bookmarking resources using del.icio.us provides a simple way into content creation in a Web 2.0 environment.

Writing a blog is a better-known way of engaging with Web 2.0 content creation tools. Technically it can be easy to set up a blog, as remotely hosted blog services such as Blogger and WordPress have very easy-to-use interfaces that allow you to set up a blog within a few minutes. However, there may be organizational barriers to setting up a blog, such as the need to ensure that any content published on behalf of the organization is approved in advance. Possible ways of overcoming such barriers include using a blog in one's own time for personal interest (which will also enhance your professional skills), using a blog within a closed environment, using a blog for a specific task or making use of micro-blogging tools, such as Twitter (www.twitter.com), which is clearly not a formal publishing tool.

Using a wiki

Since a wiki provides a collaborative environment for creating documents, it may be easier to make use of wiki software in organizations that have concerns about the use of publishing tools such as blogs. A very simple approach to making use of a wiki is to use the Google Docs service (http://docs.google.com) to create a simple document and invite colleagues to edit the document.

Google Docs can be used to collaboratively edit a document, and could be regarded as a word-processing tool rather than a wiki. The Wetpaint wiki (www.wetpaint.com) provides a more conventional approach, allowing multiple pages to be created. You can sign up for a free Wetpaint account, which could be used to support an activity in your organization. The University of Bath Library service, for example, used the Wetpaint wiki in the planning of a podcast service in the library (University of Bath).

Conclusion

Web 2.0 services are now widely available and are being widely used. They represent a development of the web, from providing a publishing environment that often required expensive content management tools and skills in either HTML authoring or specialist authoring tools, to an environment that reflects Tim Berners-Lee's original vision for the web, in which readers of the web could easily create and comment on resources.

Although there is no guarantee that individual Web 2.0 services that are popular today will continue to thrive in the future, it is probably true to say that we are unlikely to see a return to an environment that treats the user as a passive recipient of information. There is therefore a need for the library sector to have a broad understanding of the key concepts related to Web 2.0 and how Web 2.0 services may be used. This is of particular importance with respect to the development of an information literacy policy, which needs to address not only an awareness of the information needs of the user but also the needs of the user as a creator of information.

References

O'Reilly, T. (2005) *What Is Web 2.0? Design patterns and business models for the next generation of software*, www.oreillynet.com/pub/a/oreilly/tim/news/2005/09/30/what-is-web-20.html.

Radical Trust (2006) *What Is Radical Trust?*, www.radicaltrust.ca/about.

'Ray of Light' St. Joseph County Public Library Version (2003) YouTube, www.youtube.com/watch?v=vrtYdFV_Eak.

TechCrunch (2006) *Warner to License Music in YouTube Videos*, 17 September 2006, www.techcrunch.com/2006/09/17/warner-music-to-license-music-to-youtube.

University of Bath, *Library Podcast Group*, http://bathlibpod.wetpaint.com.

Part 2

Library 2.0 and the implications for IL learning

Chapter 3

Educating Web 2.0 LIS students for information literacy

SHEILA WEBBER

Introduction

Library and Information Science (LIS) students need to learn about Web 2.0 tools both in order to use them effectively themselves, and in order to use them in teaching information literacy to others. In this chapter I will discuss, first, whether LIS educators need to develop new frameworks and definitions of IL to reflect the rise of Web 2.0. I will then draw on work carried out for a European project on the LIS curriculum to identify the aspects of IL and Web 2.0 that LIS students need to address. The chapter concludes by identifying the different approaches that might be taken to enhance learning about IL using Web 2.0 tools.

What I will not do is discuss whether LIS educators need bother to incorporate Web 2.0 into the curriculum. Although specific Web 2.0 tools may come and go, it seems clear from the other chapters in this book that Web 2.0-type applications will only go away insofar as they develop into Web 3.0 applications.

IL: a new definition?

First, do we need a new definition for IL in a Web 2.0 world? Should LIS educators start by jettisoning the old definitions and trying to write new ones for their Web 2.0 or Web 3.0 students? In my view no, old definitions will do perfectly well. I will use the Chartered Institute of Library and Information Professionals' (CILIP) definition as an example. This states that

'Information literacy is knowing when and why you need information, where to find it, and how to evaluate, use and communicate it in an ethical manner' (Armstrong et al., 2005).

A key issue is how you understand the concept of 'information'. There is a substantial literature exploring and debating what information is (e.g. Capurro and Hjørland, 2003). The concept has been interpreted in many different ways, from the inclusive (communication) to the more restrictive (documents).

Commentators on IL may make the assumption that 'information' in IL definitions refers to textual information, but that is not necessarily the case. The notes on IL skills which accompany the CILIP definition make it clear that 'information may be available on paper (books, reference works, journals, magazines, newspapers, etc), digitally (on CD-ROMs, over the internet or the world wide web, on DVDs, on your own computer or network, etc.), through other media such as broadcast or film, or from a colleague or friend' (Armstrong et al., 2005).

CILIP also stresses that people need an understanding of the characteristics and merits of different types of resource, 'paper-based, electronic/digital, human, etc.', and when communicating information, one desirable skill set is 'participating effectively in collaborative writing and publication, including use of collaborative software (e.g. student group report; internal knowledge base; collaborative blog; wikipedia)' (Armstrong et al., 2005). In other words, the CILIP statement already mentions Web 2.0 tools, and the definition is flexible enough to be applied in a Web 2.0 environment. Some other definitions also explicitly refer to different channels and media for information (e.g. Johnston and Webber, 2006), but even those that do not (e.g. Information Literacy Meeting of Experts, 2003) are generally flexible enough to be interpreted with a broad definition of information.

The issue of how you define 'information' is one that is sometimes skimmed over in discussing IL with students. However, Web 2.0 makes it even more desirable to reflect on the different ways in which people acquire information and the forms information takes. In studies of information behaviour in the workplace or everyday life, family, colleagues, clients and other people emerge as vital 'sources' of information. Friends and fellow students tend to be important information sources for students in academic as well as private life. This has always been the case, but little curriculum time is normally devoted to understanding how to use people as information sources. Social networking tools and personal web presence mean that information from people you do not know personally has become easier to obtain. Thus being information literate with 'people' sources of information rises up the agenda in a Web 2.0 world.

LIS Masters courses tend to attract students from different disciplines, from chemistry to theology, which means that a LIS educator has the opportunity to draw on students' varying experiences of information when discussing IL definitions. As increasing numbers of students are engaged with one or other of the Web 2.0 social networks, it becomes easier to incorporate exercises about different information types and channels into classes. Students can draw on their own experience and reflect on how they decide whether advice from a relative, a posting from a friend on Facebook, or something written on a blog, are valid and useful information sources. This is not to say that study of more formal types of information should be dropped, rather that LIS students need to explore and understand the nature of different information types and channels.

IL: a new framework?

There are a number of frameworks or standards for IL which are used by librarians as a basis for teaching information literacy. The best known for higher education are the USA's Association of College and Research Libraries (2000) *Information Literacy Competency Standards for Higher Education*, the *Australian and New Zealand Information Literacy Framework* (Bundy, 2004) and the (United Kingdom) SCONUL (1999) Seven Pillars model. A number of models are common in the schools sector, such as the Big 6 or the American Association of School Librarians (1998) *Information Literacy Standards*.

With each of these, the basic framework can accommodate Web 2.0 tools. Take, for example, the SCONUL Seven Pillars:

1 Recognize the information need.
2 Distinguish ways of addressing the gap between what you know and what you need to know.
3 Construct strategies for extracting information from your chosen sources.
4 Locate and access the information.
5 Compare and evaluate the information.

6   Organize, apply and communicate.
7   Synthesize and create.

Someone might want to learn how to make a shirt in the virtual world Second Life. She would need to decide exactly what her information need was, for example a step-by-step description and some tips (Pillar 1), and what might be the best sources and strategies to use (Pillar 2). Sources could include looking at the Second Life wiki, searching YouTube for 'how to' videos, and asking other people for advice. The enquirer would have to work out the best ways to search and browse YouTube and the wiki: what words and phrases to use, how to formulate the search, how to browse and follow up information leads. For the 'people' sources, she would have to decide what channels to use e.g. Instant Message in Second Life itself, or use of discussion fora on the web. Then it would be a matter of using these channels in an information-literate way, for example, understanding what it was appropriate to ask, seeking out Frequently Asked Questions (Pillars 3 and 4). In evaluating the information our enquirer could use familiar criteria. Is the advice up-to-date? Have a number of people recommended this video? Is this tutorial well laid out and easy to follow? (Pillar 5). Finally, she may wish to save the information for her own future use, or add to the advice out there (for example, by augmenting a wiki entry, or by creating a video). She would need to make sure she communicated clearly and acknowledged all the sources she had used (Pillars 6 and 7).

This shows that there is nothing intrinsically Web 2.0-unfriendly about the frameworks themselves. The main problem lies in the way they tend to be elaborated and explained, with emphasis on textual, academic resources and an educational context. There is work for the relevant organizations (such as ACRL and SCONUL) in revising the more detailed guidelines that have this bias, but also for LIS educators in making sure that they use a wide range of examples when engaging LIS students with the frameworks.

Synthesis and creation used to be seen as activities which younger students would not tackle (for example, SCONUL Pillar 7 is identified with higher levels of study in the SCONUL (1999) paper). However, Web 2.0 has made publication and information combination easier. This means that ethical and legal use of information come to the foreground, as well as issues of data protection and privacy. It also means that there are exciting possibilities for encouraging people to develop their understanding of IL through creating a variety of information products.

The other aspect mentioned in some, but not all, information literacy frameworks, is working with others in an information-literate way. Developing more effective habits in sharing information, and in managing information for use within a group, are skills which are essential in many workplaces. Freely available Web 2.0 tools for sharing and aggregating information can be used to develop such skills.

What do LIS students need to learn?

Before looking at IL in a Web 2.0 context, it is worth considering IL in general. In 2005 I was part of a pan-European working group developing a chapter on what LIS students should learn about information literacy and learning (Virkus et al., 2005). This was part of a project to identify the curriculum for key LIS subjects (the pdf file which is referred to at the end of this chapter contains the whole book). I will draw on this work a fair amount in this section, since obviously it was the outcome of thoughtful discussion among educators from different European countries.

We decided that there were three key areas for LIS students:

1   To be aware of information literacy as a concept;
2   To become information literate themselves;
3   To learn about some key aspects of teaching information literacy.

(Virkus et al., 2005, 68)

This means that IL is explicitly taught. Some people in the European working party felt that, even with LIS students, the emphasis should be on teaching IL within other modules. As you will see from the final part of this chapter, I think there are good opportunities to develop LIS students' information literacy within other LIS subjects (like library marketing). However, I feel very strongly that, particularly if you are going to go on to teach IL, you need to develop your own ideas about what it means to you, how it relates to the many other 'literacies' that are talked about, where it fits in with related subjects like Knowledge Management, and so on. This should mean that you will be better able to keep developing your ideas about information literacy through life (including deciding how Web 2.0 affects information literacy).

In terms of understanding the nature of information literacy, we felt that LIS students should:

> Understand key definitions and models of IL, including similarities and differences between them;
>
> Be aware of different contexts (e.g. social life, workplace, education, private life) for information literacy, and understand the implications for IL in these different contexts;
>
> Be able to distinguish the relationship of IL with other literacies (e.g. media literacy, IT literacy) and understand the importance of basic literacy skills in underpinning IL;
>
> Understand the relationship between IL and other LIS skill and knowledge areas (e.g. Knowledge Management, Information Retrieval);
>
> Understand the research base for IL: understanding key models and theories (e.g. Bruce's . . . 7 faces model) and being aware of appropriate research approaches;
>
> Know the functions and scope of key IL organisations and initiatives in the student's country;
>
> Be aware of the history and origins of IL.
>
> (Virkus et al., 2005, 71–2)

I think it is a good idea for students to use one of the IL frameworks to reflect on their own IL, for example as a structure for reflecting on their IL development through a course. They are then better placed to critique the framework. Is it valid and helpful when reflecting on IL activities based around Web 2.0 tools? If not, why not? If there are problems, are they to do with the framework, or with the students' own assumptions or interpretation of the framework, or the lecturer's approach to the subject? Can students find examples on the web or in the literature that use the framework successfully? What are students' and practitioners' opinions?

Even if you end up in an organization where the term 'information literacy' is called something else (e.g. personal information management or information fluency) it is still useful to have this basis of knowledge and understanding. It means that you may find it easier to present the most acceptable definition and framework for IL-under-another-name, you would be better placed to tie it into other organizational initiatives and fads, and you should be aware of IL work that has been done in similar contexts.

As already mentioned, the onus is on the IL educator to encourage LIS students to explore IL in different contexts, and not just textual information in educational settings. Since even LIS students are assessment driven to some extent, this also means devising assessments which require students to practise information literacy skills which are not entirely focused on academic and textual resources.

When it comes to librarians' skills in teaching IL, the European working party identified four main areas for learning:

1   Curriculum design and planning (one of the elements listed here is understanding appropriate use of technology in designing learning environments).
2   Understanding learners and learning theory (which includes understanding e-learning models and the needs of e-learners).
3   Understanding basic concepts, theories and practice of teaching.
4   Understanding the context for teaching and learning (e.g. issues concerned with the teaching and learner-support role of the librarian).

Learning to teach using Web 2.0 tools fits within these four areas: there is increasing consensus that 'good strategies for e-learning' are part of 'good strategies for learning', so that teaching with technology should not be seen as a strange and separate activity. It is always valuable to learn more about specific tools, to put theory into practice. However, technology changes so fast that it is more crucial to learn some of the underlying concepts. Thus you can develop an approach to teaching that enables you to evaluate new tools and see how they can been used effectively in learning and teaching.

One problem for LIS educators is fitting everything that needs to be taught into the curriculum. This is a particular challenge in those countries, like the UK, where the Masters course is only twelve months long. The teaching and learning agenda listed above is a whole Masters programme in itself, and so in many courses (including those offered by my own department) some elements may be included in core classes, but others are likely to be covered as options. However, given the relevance of Web 2.0 to different areas of library and information work, the use of Web 2.0 tools in teaching information literacy is probably more likely to be covered than some aspects of educational theory.

Approaches to teaching LIS students

As already indicated, there are three ways in which Web 2.0 has an impact on LIS students:

- in developing students' own ideas about what IL means
- in affecting the knowledge and skills the students need to learn in order to become information literate themselves
- in providing more tools and opportunities for designing IL courses and activities for other learners.

I have already talked about some of the ways in which students can be engaged in the first two, and made it clear that I think there needs to be some space in the curriculum where the teacher facilitates students' understanding of information literacy, introduces key ideas and concepts and challenges students to question and develop their ideas of what IL means.

Students need to develop their abilities to be information literate with Web 2.0 tools. This means learning to be comfortable with the basic technology (but not necessarily delving deep into the technical side unless that is an area you want to specialize in), learning what kinds of function you can expect in different tools, and what they are useful for, and gaining confidence in using and evaluating information via different tools.

At the moment there seems to be a trend towards identifying Web 2.0 as a separate topic, and leading students through an exploration of different tools. This trend is most obvious in the 23 Things projects at different libraries which, at time of writing, have developed from (in the USA) the Public Library of Charlotte and Mecklenburg County's (2007) Learning 2.0 Program and (in Australia), Murdoch University Library's (2006) MULTA project. The online Five Weeks to a Social Library (Farkas et al., 2007) course is also influential. These continuing professional development (CPD) initiatives introduce library staff to different Web 2.0 tools, and then set tasks which involve participants in using the tools and reflecting on their practical application in the workplace. For example, in the University of Michigan Library's (2007) MLibrary 2.0 programme, activities include joining Facebook, so you can 'Consider how the library could use Facebook for outreach or for reference; make a wall or discussion post about your thoughts in the MLibrary2.0 [Facebook] group.'

One of the weaknesses of this approach is that it can focus attention on the specific tool, rather than its relationship with other aspects of library work and other (non-Web 2.0) tools. In a CPD context this may be fine: each participant is in a specific and familiar context and can relate the Web 2.0 tools to that. Students on LIS courses, however, will be graduating into a wide variety of workplaces, and trying to draw in examples from different sectors may make a 'Web 2.0' course frustratingly bitty.

It certainly cannot be assumed that students (even younger ones) will just 'pick up' skills in making videos, managing blogs, convening meetings in a virtual world, or embedding current awareness applications in Facebook. Using blended learning techniques and facilitating learning between peers are obviously in the spirit of Web 2.0, but need careful planning and facilitation. Beyond that, the way in which LIS students' Web 2.0 skills are developed will depend on the structure and specialist focus of a particular LIS course. So, for example, a course in which Knowledge Management is a key element might incorporate learning about Web 2.0 tools into activities concerning communities of practice, knowledge sharing and knowledge elicitation. On courses where library management and marketing are core elements, different tools might be used (for example) to compile a wiki on management practices observed in library visits, or to create a Facebook or Second Life presence for the library, or to produce a video about customers' perceptions of service quality.

In fact most of the examples above can also be seen from an information literacy perspective. The management wiki would involve identifying the precise kind of information needed, students might gather factual information about the visited libraries to provide context, evaluate the information before deciding what to put in the wiki, develop guidelines for submitting observations from visits, organize the information effectively, and take account of ethical issues when presenting opinions.

As regards learning how to teach using Web 2.0 tools, this can be incorporated into an information literacy class (with students using the tools to develop guides or tutorials for each other, and evaluating existing Web 2.0-based tutorials). More obviously, Web 2.0 tools can be created and evaluated as part of a class about learning and teaching. Creating and/or evaluating a Web 2.0-based product such as a tutorial can constitute assessed work.

The only caveat in this area is that the lecturer needs to be confident that the student's work will not suddenly disappear before assessment is complete. While a number of free Web 2.0 tools seem reliable, it is not fair on students to take risks with their work, and this can make educators cautious about using free Web 2.0 resources as vehicles for assessment.

Conclusion

There is no need for every LIS graduate to become a Web 2.0 guru. However, all LIS professionals have to be able to engage critically with new online tools in order to identify their potential in their own LIS specialism. LIS managers also need to spot those Web 2.0 tools that will enable them, and their organization, to manage resources more effectively. Therefore all LIS graduates need to feel comfortable in using whatever web tools are prominent at the time they are studying, and to feel confident that they will be able to keep track of web developments and be capable of assessing them.

This provides challenges to LIS educators in revising the curriculum: not just subject content, but the way in which the curriculum is delivered. Librarianship and Information Management are constantly developing subjects, so having to make changes every year is nothing new. However, it certainly does not get any easier to put together a curriculum that covers what employers demand, is up to date without being superficially trendy, is appropriately challenging for an academic programme (yet practical enough to appeal to future professionals) and pedagogically innovative and engaging. I think that all LIS educators are aware that this is what we have to do, though, to meet the needs of the profession.

There is a Web 2.0 challenge for professional associations and for employers too. Professional associations should be helping professionals in their continuing professional development, as well as setting an example in the use of Web 2.0. Employers also need to help their staff learn on the job, and this can be done, as is demonstrated by the 23 Things initiatives mentioned above.

Web 2.0 can be a bonus as well as a challenge, making learning and teaching more interesting (and even fun) for everyone. It requires some effort and flexibility in keeping up with this year's web trends, but the rewards are great, to keep LIS, and LIS professionals, at the centre of the information society.

References

American Association of School Librarians (1998) *Information Literacy Standards for Student Learning: standards and indicators,* American Library Association, www.ala.org/ala/aasl/aaslproftools/informationpower/ InformationLiteracyStandards_final.pdf.

Armstrong, C., Boden, D., Town, S., Woolley, M., Webber, S. and Abell, A. (2005) CILIP Defines Information Literacy for the UK, *Library and Information Update,* **4** (1), 22–5, www.cilip.org.uk/publications/updatemagazine/archive/ archive2005/janfeb/armstrong.htm.

Association of College and Research Libraries (2000) *Information Literacy Competency Standards for Higher Education,* American Library Association, www.ala.org/ala/acrl/acrlstandards/informationliteracycompetency.htm.

Bundy, A. (ed.) (2004) *Australian and New Zealand Information Literacy Framework: principles, standards and practice,* 2nd edn, Australian and New Zealand Institute for Information Literacy, www.anziil.org/resources.

Capurro, R. and Hjørland, B. (2003) The Concept of Information. In Cronin, B. (ed.), *Annual Review of Information Science and Technology (ARIST),* **37,** Information Today.

Farkas, M. et al. (2007) Five Weeks to a Social Library, www.sociallibraries.com/course.

Information Literacy Meeting of Experts (2003) *The Prague Declaration: towards an information literate society,* NCLIS, www.nclis.gov/libinter/infolitconf&meet/post-infolitconf&meet/ post-infolitconf&meet.html.

Johnston, B. and Webber, S. (2006) As We May Think: information literacy as a discipline for the information age, *Research Strategies,* **20** (3), 108–21.

Murdoch University Library (2006) *Murdoch University Thinking Aloud,* http://carcit.library.curtin.edu.au/index.php/MULTA:Murdoch_ University_Library_Thinking_Aloud.

Public Library of Charlotte and Mecklenburg County (2007) Learning 2.0, http://plcmcl2-about.blogspot.com.

SCONUL (1999) *Information Skills in Higher Education: a SCONUL position paper,* www.sconul.ac.uk/groups/information_literacy/papers/Seven_pillars2.pdf.

University of Michigan Library (2007) *About MLibrary 2.0,* www.lib.umich.edu/lib20/index.html.

Virkus, S. et al. (2005) Information Literacy and Learning. In Kajberg, L. and
    Lørring, L. (eds), *European Curriculum: reflections on library and information
    science education*, The Royal School of Library and Information Science,
    http://biblis.db.dk/uhtbin/hyperion.exe/db.leikaj05.

Chapter 4

School Library 2.0: new skills, new knowledge, new futures

JUDY O'CONNELL

Introduction

Libraries have been an integral part of civilization – providing a ponderous archive of knowledge and lasting record of the human spirit. From Alexandria to the present, a key purpose of libraries has been to store information and be a place of research and learning. Fast forward to the 20th century, when drawing on this heritage we saw the emergence of school libraries positioned right at the centre of learning for our children and young adults.

From such an august heritage, our school libraries have shown their value and purpose many times over, and their successes have been recorded through personal experiences and research studies. There are many school library impact studies (Library Research Service, 2007), the best known being the Colorado Studies, which prove that school libraries have a direct link to student achievement. We know that school libraries make a difference to student learning (International Association of School Librarianship, 2007).

Two elements of a school library have stood the test of time. The first has been to nurture literacy and promote the pleasure of reading. The second has been to provide pathways to information and knowledge by promoting information literacy skills and processes. The point is that school libraries have a distinct function and purpose, both similar to and different from other libraries, which draws on past, present and future possibilities in that unique school library mix of the literary, cultural, recreational, and research needs of our 'learner' students.

The school library provides an organizational and educational centre for students and teachers striving to meet the demands of modern learning and the requirements of the learning programmes outlined by local authorities or governments. What is it about learning that is changing the scope of the school library's function and purpose? What does it mean to be a teacher librarian, a school librarian or school media specialist in a Web 2.0 world?

The internet is undergoing a transformation. The net is a child in terms of the maturation of information technology, and in its current evolution to the 'semantic web' with its emerging methods of information extraction, concept tracking and semantic analysis of data. Consequently our approaches to information literacy have to change – no question!

Functioning in a Web 2.0 world

Marc Prensky (2006) calls today's students 'digital natives'. Raised with an easy familiarity with video games, e-mail, instant messaging, MySpace and other Web 2.0 social networking habits, they have developed patterns of engagement that are different from those of earlier generations. Educators must recognize these differences and develop school library services that are appropriate in depth and diversity.

Web 2.0 tools are important, but their impact goes much deeper than their networking novelty might suggest. The tools for information seeking and the spaces for information sharing are rapidly changing and developing.

Johnson (2006) considers that there are three critical societal changes that impact on libraries' survival and opportunities to thrive:

- the growing digitization and portability of information
- emerging fundamental changes in the nature and sources of information
- the critical need for new skills for workers in a global economy.

In its 2.0 incarnation, the digitally re-shifted school library must transcend the physical space to bring services and programming to every student and teacher throughout the school, wherever learning takes place in new spaces and places, to prepare our students for the digital world of work.

Challenges and opportunities

Web 2.0 social networking makes participation fast. Our students are living that connection and driving Web 2.0 transformation. It is often teenagers or those in their twenties who create revolutionary new social networking tools such as YouTube, Facebook, WordPress and more. This is confirmed by research reported by Business Week (2007), which indicates that there are significantly more people aged from 12 to 26 years than older groups who are 'creators' 'critics' and 'joiners' – in other words, who publish web pages, write blogs, upload videos to sites like YouTube; who comment on blogs and post ratings and reviews; and who are members of social networking sites like MySpace or Bebo. So we must ask ourselves just how Web 2.0 can support our school's learning and teaching agenda – because if we do not, it threatens to make the difference between teachers and learners more acute than ever.

On the other hand, by embracing a Web 2.0 mindset we just might close the gap. This mindset will include accepting a transition from formal to informal learning spaces; accepting a shift from whole class to personalized learning opportunities; and accepting a change from restrictive and constructed learning activities to creative and extended learning opportunities. In all these instances the learner (Web 2.0 style) is the author of personal creativity, knowledge and understanding.

In other words, flexibility and personalization are at the core of re-purposing information literacy instruction in a Web 2.0 world. If students think about the internet as a virtual locker, backpack, notebook, diary and communication tool, then we must create flexible learning environments that support the use of multiple bibliographic and digital resource tools, including Web 2.0. In such a context our information literacy instruction framework needs to be personalized, real, physical, virtual and even visceral. This is very different. But in a Web 2.0 world our students must be passionate about their personalized learning, and it is the role of school librarians to help make it so.

Smart tools, smart research

The information literacy dilemma starts with the word 'find'. Searching is an essential skill for any generation – but more so for the Google generation. Have you noticed the primacy of Google in the minds of students? Have you been told that libraries don't matter because we have Google? Students of all ages are heavy Google users, despite the existence of many other and more specialized search engines. 'The disturbing reality is that the internet is replete with out-of-date, conflicting, and inaccurate information. Rumor mills abound, and even trustworthy sites can be slow at updating facts and figures, leaving both "Googler" and "Googlee" exasperated' (Vise, 2005,147).

Valenza (2006) explains that young information seekers do not have the sophisticated skills or understanding needed to navigate complex information environments and to evaluate the information that they find. Students prefer natural language searching. Couple this with difficulties in identifying information needs in environments that require appropriate terminology or vocabulary in search interfaces, and it becomes clear that we have a potentially 'dangerous' problem.

So the first challenge in the Web 2.0 information literacy environment is the matter of search. While we may have considered that we addressed searching successfully – by teaching students to use a range of search engines (including advanced and Boolean searching) and then to analyse the authority of the sites and sources they visit online in order to determine the value of the information found – we really have only just begun.

Working with search software in a school library has become critically important. At the school level there may be a library system, content or learning management system, a system for distributing videos and other multimedia, and more. In all of these the school librarian needs to consider how to develop the library catalogue or information retrieval systems, and how to define the required metadata so that automated capabilities of these systems allow students to easily find the resources they need to support their learning. By reverse-engineering organizational information structures to match the information literacy strategies that support students' information-seeking habits, school librarians can really make a difference and encourage good information literacy habits in their students at the school level.

In a Library 2.0 world it has become essential to work more closely with technology to enhance information retrieval and to look beyond existing structures and forms of information organization. Subject indexes are no longer sufficient in an environment where students expect (rightly or wrongly) to get easy answers to complex questions.

Library systems are notoriously unfriendly, seemingly designed for the expert rather than the user. At the simplest level consider aligning keywords to terms used in subject and knowledge disciplines, and then linking these key terms as 'non-preferred' or 'See' terms within your library catalogue. In other words, develop your subject indexes to reflect real learning needs unique to your students. Utilize the knowledge expertise of your teachers and the practical usage of your students to enhance your existing taxonomy. You have to do this to align your system to the flexible mindset that is Web 2.0.

Then turn your focus to all areas where information is to be retrieved. Does your school have a recommended thesaurus of terms for information organization in its digital repository or video repository? What metadata does it include? Do you know what you could do to optimize search for files and information across your school's content management system? (Think Knowledge Management here!)

Does your library system import metadata for other sources included in your catalogue, for example web resources, image repositories, learning objects, e-books, audio-books and other content enrichment such as those provided by Syndetic solutions (www.syndetics.com)? When any of these resources are blended into a library information system, school librarians need to consider information literacy requirements for students and adapt indexing options to facilitate information access and information retrieval.

Schools are also providing access to many different digital and online resources, often on a subscription basis. Has your library incorporated 'federated searching' (the ability to simultaneously search multiple data sources) into your library catalogue or information system? Once again, decisions at the institutional level have an impact on the nature of information literacy interactions in your school, and the type of training and personalized learning support that is made available.

The answers to these questions will inform the nature of the structures that you build in your school and school library in order to embrace an information literacy teaching model that represents Web 2.0 search usability and functionality.

Search engines – one model for all?

Mitchell (2007) has reiterated that searching for information is more than just a rules-driven process, and that there is no one correct way to search for information in this diverse Web 2.0 landscape. It is the big picture processes, not the intricacies of a single interface (that could change at any time), that we need to take into consideration.

Our duty as teachers of information literacy is to help develop learners who can adapt both with and as a result of knowledge in each new learning situation. A school librarian need only visit Pandia Powersearch and their 'all-in-one' list of search engines (www.pandia.com/powersearch/index.html) in order to be prompted to develop new ways to help students learn how to incorporate alternative search strategies into their personal information-seeking toolkit – and then work with teachers to integrate deeper understanding about search strategies into the fabric of the learning and teaching experiences in the school.

Better still, school librarians can use their new knowledge of searching, Web 2.0 style, by showing students how to 'roll their own' search from resources they trust using Rollyo (www.rollyo.com) or build their own Google search engine (http://google.com/coop/cse) or Yahoo Search builder (http://builder.search.yahoo.com/m/promo) for specifically targeted information needs. Teaching students to identify their information need and shape the discovery of information with a Web 2.0 approach empowers the learner, rather than reducing learning to a quick-fix, 'cut and paste' option.

Of course, a school librarian can also adopt these tools to effectively support the information-literate Web 2.0 school community. For example, building a topic search tool or book review finder, and incorporating this tailored search tool right into the school library website or the school library blog, is a proactive information-literate strategy to support the developing information literacy skills of students.

These very simple strategies are the new face of search in Web 2.0 information literacy. They require a shift of thinking from simply developing a search strategy to understanding search engines, and then using the power of Web 2.0 to make your own search strategy come to life. It can then be embedded into another Web 2.0 tool such as a blog or wiki (which may be created for a particular unit of work, or to support a particular requirement for the learning and teaching needs at your school).

As part of the information literacy toolkit, school librarians should also familiarize students with the differences between natural language, visual, clustering or metadata search engines in order to appreciate 'Search 2.0' versus traditional search as explained by Ezzy (2006). Remember to explain to your students about the tools available for searching the deep end of the web for information that can only be found by very specific and direct queries (Turner, 2006; Trinity College, 2007).

Smart tools and smart research will make information literacy search strategies in Library 2.0 an essential learning experience for students. Teach them how to search – but only after you have taught yourself how to improve search functionality within your institution and beyond!

Flexibility, folksonomy and favourites

It's clear that flexibility is a critical component of Library 2.0, and comes in a number of guises. The whole point is to keep students 'on task' engaging with learning, and collaborating with teachers and other learners in the process.

Blogs and wikis provide ideal flexible environments which allow for asynchronous collaboration, and learning in a global context. Synchronous communication is also possible in a learning setting using collaboration tools such as Elluminate, or by embedding communication widgets into wikis and blogs, for instant messaging, or tools like Meebo, Twitter or more. Stephens (2006) describes a wealth of tools and ideas for best practices using Web 2.0 social software. Bradley's conference presentation (2007) provides a neat summary of Library 2.0 possibilities. Richardson (2007) tells about one of the earliest and best school library blogs from Galileo High School in San Francisco, where the librarian uses a 'Li-Blog-ary' to identify resources for classes, update the school community on new offerings, link to online databases and publish student reviews. If you are still not convinced, explore the Blogging Libraries Wiki for more, and see how others have incorporated these ideas. Among them Dr Charles Best Secondary School Library, and Delany Library are excellent examples. Investigate the various widgets that are used to enhance information access and communication options for the students.

What a good 'school librarian 2.0' needs to do is to incorporate Web 2.0 tools into the information dissemination framework while modelling exemplary information literacy strategies for students and teachers. Most school librarians will begin this adventure by starting a book blog, or a project wiki. The Horizon Project (2007) successfully show-cased the collaborative learning potential in these Web 2.0 environments. While the assessment rubrics include information literacy concepts, clear scaffolding of development of information literacy skills and competences is not included. So even such a wonderfully creative project would benefit from Web 2.0 information literacy guidance from the school librarian.

One of the easiest yet most critical areas for Library 2.0 operations is in the field of 'taxonomy' in the new generation version, known as 'folksonomy' and used for social bookmarking and 'tagging' information in shared online spaces. Tags are a means for individuals to organize and describe resources in personally meaningful language and classification schemes. Tagging is a bottom-up, grass-roots phenomenon, in which users classify resources with searchable keywords. The tags are free-form labels chosen by the user, not selected from a controlled vocabulary. For the first time in history, students and teachers can sort and organize information 'naturally' and online, thus organizing and managing information for personal use or with groups of learners. Godwin-Jones (2006) elaborates on tagging and the semantic web (which provides a common framework that allows data to be shared and re-used across application, enterprise, and community boundaries), and in so doing highlights the fact that the tagging process is by no means simply technical – a way of categorizing resources. It also has a strong social dimension, as users of the site find common interests and create online communities.

Show information literacy students how to 'tag' and manage bookmarks with del.icio.us, Furl, Magnolia or others; make annotations on web pages with Clipmarks or Wiz; and use these tools to organize their sources, share their collaborative project information, manage their personal knowledge repository, and tie this information via a widget to their blogs and wikis. In addition to being a popular way of organizing resources, tags enable the formation of unexpected connections with others sharing similar interests. Use tagging for photosharing (Flickr, Photobucket), podcasting (iTunes, Podomatic, Podbean), videosharing (YouTube, TeacherTube), slide sharing (SlideShare, Slidecast), and so on.

The Horizon project (2007) made excellent use of distributed information using tagging, sharing resources across the globe with the tag 'hz07' in the social bookmarking site del.icio.us and video-sharing site YouTube. It was easy for global participants in the project to provide 24/7 support by using this tag. School libraries are also embracing this collaborative method of sharing web resources, with school librarians and teachers establishing social bookmarking as a library service or service to a particular project team or school year group.

What tagging highlights (since it applies to a large range of interfaces) is the need for supporting students with information literacy strategies that are multi-modal and collaborative in nature – and which embrace the natural language functionality of folksonomy.

RSS that information need

RSS is definitely changing the web, changing our classrooms and changing the information literacy needs of our students. Because students need to access both traditional and emerging sources of information, both formal and informal, RSS needs to be part of their information literacy toolkit and the toolkit of school librarians.

Utilize RSS feeds to assist students to subscribe to journal collections, media sites and other information sources, as well as to your library's blog, book lists, photo collections, videos, podcasts and more. It is essential to provide students with information skills training in how to maximize the use of RSS feeds for information gathering and sharing.

Collaboration is the key. Have your students subscribe to their fellow students' blogs or wikis; or have teachers subscribe to students' work and related sources. However, the power of RSS comes into its own with web-based information aggregators such as Pageflakes, iGoogle, Netvibes or other choices. Web 2.0 educator Will Richardson shares his 'flake' at www.pageflakes. com/weblogged.ashx, which also has an excellent demonstration of this RSS tool for topic aggregation on the Darfur tab. The information is dynamic, constantly updated and shows what's happening in Darfur and in other parts of the world in response. RSS pages of this type can be pretty effective for gathering content, making it easier to make decisions about what to do with that content.

The natural extension of this concept is for libraries to 'mashup' and enrich their OPAC with maps, reviews, jacket images, or folksonomies – though this is not common in school libraries yet. Blyberg (2006) demonstrates the power and flexibility of API programming in creating mashups with his Go-go Google Gadget. At any rate, the development of products for collecting and organizing data continues. For example, Second Brain (your personal internet library), at www.secondbrain.com, allows users to aggregate all their creations, services and favourites, and then share and/or publish them online. Capturing data is easy, and all existing tags, comments and thumbnails are manageable and easily identifiable ones. Second Brain looks at Web 2.0 as a widely distributed desktop, albeit a huge one. What a significant area of development for school librarians – a personal library, resource and research space for each student.

School librarians can use RSS to deliver professional learning programmes, as well as news and information. The thing about RSS is that it goes both ways – providing school librarians (and students) with a Web 2.0 tool with almost limitless opportunities for blending knowledge and information sources, organizing them, and having them ready for the rich learning tasks as set out by the teacher or school librarian.

Build your support for information literacy programmes

Of course, in order to promote an information-literate school community, school librarians (in a Web 2.0 world) need to develop online tutorials, videos (for YouTube for example), audio podcasts, slideshows and more, so that students will have access to these as part of their personalized skill-development toolkit. Even a small school library can create a free Group space in TeacherTube, or embed a podbean audio compilation into a library blog (also hosted free on edublogs or blogger).

School librarians also need to create social networking spaces as virtual learning and collaboration spaces. School librarians are active members of many online spaces, such as Facebook, Ning or Twitter. Librarians and their professional associations are embracing the possibilities, as demonstrated by the School Library Learning 2.0 project of the California School Library Association. These and other social networking sites provide the ideal way to create a learning community, for a few or many engaged in a rich learning task, where they can share and collaborate with ease 24/7.

The Web 2.0 options are fun, engaging – and most certainly extend the range of information literacy instruction needs we have to meet for our net-savvy students. So, school librarians, in collaboration with teachers, need to ensure that they are facilitating information literacy programmes in this 2.0 environment that allow them to learn independently and in ways that allow students to engage with expert guides and mentors in order to have their information literacy needs addressed. Students need the support of *guided enquiry* – the intervention of an instructional team of school librarians and teachers to guide students through curriculum-based enquiry units that build deep knowledge and deep understanding of a curriculum topic, and gradually lead towards independent learning (Kuhlthau and Todd, 2007).

What does Web 2.0 really mean for school libraries? As we create conversations, connections and a Web 2.0 learning community, we are opening the door to a better school library future – one that embraces the digital identity of our students and their multi-modal minds. We need to look for new ways of working with literacy, information literacy and digital fluency. School libraries need to embrace Web 2.0 and change the focus and purpose of information services. In so doing, our new learning communities will be able to get involved in responsive academic discourse and new processes and products will emerge, leading to new forms of digital scholarship and personalized learning.

References

Blyberg, J. (2006) *Go-go Google Gadget*, Blyberg.net, www.blyberg.net/2006/08/18/go-go-google-gadget.

Bradley, P. (2007) *Web 2.0: implications for your library*, School Library Association's Slidespace, www.slideshare.net/SLA/web-20-implications-for-your-library.

Business Week Magazine (2007) *Chart: who participates and what people are doing online*, www.businessweek.com/magazine/content/07_24/b4038405.htm (11 June).

Ezzy, E. (2006) *Search 2.0 versus Traditional Search: Parts 1 and 2*, Read/WriteWeb, www.readwriteweb.com/archives/search_20_vs_tr.php.

Godwin-Jones, R. (2006) Emerging Technologies: tag clouds in the blogosphere, electronic literacy and social networking, *Language, Learning and Technology*, **10** (2), http://llt.msu.edu/vol10num2/pdf/emerging.pdf.

Horizon Project (2007), http://horizonproject.wikispaces.com.

International Association of School Librarianship (2007) *School Libraries Make a Difference to Student Achievement*, www.iasl-online.org/advocacy/make-a-difference.html.

Johnson, D. (2006) *Dangers and Opportunities: challenges for libraries in the digital age*, www.doug-johnson.com/storage/handouts/danger.pdf.

Kuhlthau, C. and Todd, R. (2007) *Guided Inquiry*, Center for International Scholarship in School Libraries at Rutgers University, www.cissl.scils.rutgers.edu/guided_inquiry/introduction.html.

Library Research Service (2007) *School Library Impact Studies*, www.lrs.org/impact.php.

Mitchell, P. (2007) *Information Literacy Experts or Expats?* SLANZA Conference
www.educationau.edu.au/jahia/webdav/site/myjahiasite/shared/papers/
slanza_pm.pdf.

Prensky, M. (2006) Listen to the Natives, *Educational Leadership,* **63** (4)
(December 2005/January 2006), 8–13,
www.ascd.org/authors/ed_lead/el200512_prensky.html.

Richardson, W. (2007) Online-Powered School Libraries: Web 2.0 technologies
are transforming the school library, *District Administration: The Magazine for
K12 Leaders* (January),
www.districtadministration.com/viewarticle.aspx?articleid=1055.

Stephens, M. (2006) *Web 2.0 and Libraries: best practices for social software,*
Library Technology Reports: expert guides to library systems and services,
ALA TechSource, **42** (4) (July/August).

Trinity College (2007) *Invisible or Deep Web Search Engines,* P. L. Duffy Resource
Centre, www.trinity.wa.edu.au/plduffyrc/web/invis/invisible.htm.

Turner, L. (2006) *Delving into the Deep End of the Web,* TechLearning,
www.techlearning.com/story/showArticle.jhtml?articleID=181503756.

Valenza, J. (2006) They Might be Gurus: teen information-seeking behaviour,
E-Voya, (April),
http://pdfs.voya.com/VO/YA2/VOYA200604T9gTeamTech.pdf.

Vise, D. (2005) *The Google Story,* Pan Books.

Helpful resources

Blogging Libraries Wiki: School libraries
www.blogwithoutalibrary.net/links/index.php?title=School_libraries.

HeyJude, http://heyjude.wordpress.com.

Judy's Library 2.0 del.icio.us collection, http://del.icio.us/heyjude/Library2.0.

Library 2.0 Matrix, www.flickr.com/photos/heyjude/230640507.

School Library Learning 2.0, http://schoollibrarylearning2.blogspot.com.

Teacher Librarian Network, http://teacherlibrarian.ning.com.

Teacher Librarian Wiki, http://teacherlibrarianwiki.pbwiki.com.

Chapter 5

Information literacy, Web 2.0 and public libraries: an exploration

MICHELLE McLEAN

Introduction

Web 2.0 has brought new challenges, and new means of offering services and content. Public librarians are exploring how these tools can be used, always with the ultimate aim of providing the best services to their users, including continuing opportunities for lifelong learning. Now more than ever, library users are virtual visitors as well as physical, so it is even more important that public libraries are 'virtually' up to date and present, to serve our users when they are in virtual spaces.

Information literacy is a much broader area in public libraries than in other sectors, with no officially defined or assigned responsibilities (Skov, 2004; Lewis, n.d). However, public libraries are aware of the need to explore IL with our users and as far as we are able, we teach information literacy to our communities. Whether it be through class visits, speaking to local groups, seminars in-house, making learning materials available (e.g. helpsheets on using the catalogue) or just one-to-one instruction, public libraries recognize the important role they play in lifelong learning in their communities.

With my continuing interest in virtual library services as a background, I applied for a Ramsay and Reid Scholarship[1] from the State Library of Victoria, Australia, to undertake a study tour of US public libraries and their virtual services. I was awarded the scholarship in November 2006 and conducted the study tour in April 2007, including in the trip the Computers in Libraries 2007 conference in Washington DC. As I travelled, I posted nightly on my blog Connecting Librarian.[2] Much of what you will read in this chapter comes from that tour and my knowledge of the public library scene in Victoria, Australia.

For those who do not yet have an awareness of Web 2.0 tools, public libraries have an informal responsibility to help them learn. For many in our communities, the public library is their only source of internet access and one of the few accessible resources they have for lifelong learning. Many of our users will learn about Web 2.0 through the resources public libraries provide. This can be through formal classes teaching the use of computers and general or specific desktop and internet applications (including Web 2.0 tools), or through our use of these tools to communicate with, inform and educate our communities.

Web 2.0 tools for public librarians

Before we can utilize Web 2.0 technologies to serve our users, we have to be aware of them. Before we can provide information literacy to our users, we have to be information literate ourselves. The irony is that the best way of learning about Web 2.0 tools is via Web 2.0 tools. Fortunately there are many librarians already utilizing tools such as blogs, wikis and podcasts to up-skill themselves and other librarians.

The best known such programme is Learning 2.0[3] from the Public Library of Charlotte and Mecklenburg County in North Carolina, USA. Created by Technology Director Helene Blowers, it has been made available to anyone who wants to use it, through a Creative Commons licence. The programme aims to expose library staff to new Web 2.0 tools through the use of a blog, podcasts and play, in as little as 20 minutes per week. Learning 2.0 is a blog-based, self-paced learning programme, which usually runs for nine weeks, with an extra four weeks for catch up or exploration time. It uses free Web 2.0 tools to provide content, so there is no hardware or software cost to run the programme.

In the first week, participants are required to set up their own blog, which they can do anonymously if they choose, and from then on, to blog about their discoveries as they move through the programme. The programme gives participants an introduction to blogs, image sharing, RSS and news-readers, image generators, LibraryThing and customizable search tools, tagging and folksonomies, wikis, online applications and tools, podcasts, videos and downloadable audio.

The programme has been picked up and quite often adapted to local conditions by libraries around the world. To help library staff get interested and involved in the programme, libraries have used incentives, such as giving USB memory sticks to all those who complete the programme, or the chance to win an MP3 player. Libraries are also using the programme's training format for further exposure to Web 2.0 tools and expanding it into other areas of library staff training, including databases and core computer competencies. For example, the Public Library of Charlotte and Mecklenburg County has moved on to Learning 2.1[4] where each month they explore other uses of Web 2.0 tools, including such things as scrapbooking, mini-blogging and online file storage.

Meredith Farkas from the University of Norwich (Vermont, USA) used a wiki to provide another resource of great benefit to library staff: Library Success, a best practices wiki, aims to be a 'one-stop shop for great ideas and information for all types of librarians'.[5] An open resource, to which any librarian can contribute, it gives great ideas and outlines successful programmes, tips and other information on a range of topics, including community, management, collection development, professional development programmes, readers' advisory, information services and information literacy, marketing, services to specific groups, technology and collaboration. Although the content is not exclusively relevant to public libraries, there is much that has come from public libraries and much more that could be adapted to the public library environment. Contributions are welcome and encouraged, so libraries can learn from others' experiences.

Blogs

Blogs have been the Web 2.0 tool most often adopted by public libraries. Blogs have a range of hosting options, from free blog sites such as Blogger, to web-hosted or self-hosted options like WordPress, which make them very appealing to public libraries which don't often have a lot of technical expertise available in-house.

Blogs also give public libraries a new, exciting and easy-to-use means of communicating with their users and more importantly, when comments are enabled, allowing their users to communicate back. Blogs are also flexible in that they can be used in a general way, or many can be used, each with a specific, more narrow focus.

Darien Library[6] in Connecticut, USA, have ten blogs on their website, each with a very different focus. They have blogs on the topics of Books, Music and Movies, From the Director, Children's, Teens, Technology, Front desk, New Building, Events and Community Matters. Their Director's blog is written by the Library Director, Louise Parker Berry, who communicates in a personal way with Darien Library users and gives them a chance to feed back straight to the top. Each blog is administered by a library staff member and is updated weekly, giving users new content to explore on a regular basis. RSS feeds from each blog are fed into the home page and newsletter, which is e-mailed out to users, thereby giving their blog content even greater exposure.

Ann Arbor District Library in Michigan, USA, have a blog-based website.[7] Using the Drupal content management system (CMS), all information on their website is generated using blogs and associated software. Their home page comprises RSS feeds from their various blogs and all staff are able to blog, with their manager's approval and after a short training session. In the two years since the library website was launched in this form, they have had over 10,000 comments on their blog posts. The most popular blog has been on gaming, a big gaming community having developed there. This blog hosts thriving conversations which in turn generate a lot of interest in and support for their gaming events.

Thomas Ford Memorial Library in Illinois, USA, have used a blog in a project with their partner, the Western Springs Historical Society.[8] They have used this blog to post historical photos with brief information on each. Comments have been enabled, allowing users to post further information about these properties, including dates, past residents, changes and more. Each post has been tagged with the street name, which enables users to search for properties on a given street. As with all blogs, it is searchable, thereby making the information more widely accessible.

Eastern Regional Libraries in Melbourne, Australia, have replaced their teen web page with a blog with links to some static pages.[9] They are using their blog for teen-generated reviews of books, CDs and games. Although the blog is not open for anyone to write to it, reviews are easily posted to it, having been submitted via a form linked from the blog. The reviews are searchable and people are able to respond with comments, making it potentially more a discussion than just a review.

These are just some of the ways that public libraries are using blogs. There are many more library blogs out there and many more ways that libraries can use them. Blogs are an easy-to-use communication tool that all public libraries should be using, for promotion as well as for information literacy. As the examples outlined show, they can be used to learn about library materials and local history and to learn from reviews, with users having the opportunity to participate and share their own information and viewpoints via comments. Many libraries use blogs to inform users of their electronic resources and the best ways to use them. Blogs are also used to share other information literacy skills, although the skills are not often explicitly described as such. Some of these include how to assess the validity of electronic content, find the best resources to use, discover what makes them the best and much more.

RSS feeds

Although typically related to blogs and podcasts, RSS feeds can also be generated from other content sources. Public libraries are using RSS in innovative ways to make the current content that users want available to them in a timely manner.

Hennepin County Public Library offer RSS feeds[10] to their library news, to their subject guides, catalogue news, events and classes, booklists, customized searches and to their users' library accounts – so users know what they have on loan and on hold. Princeton Public Library's Book Lovers' Wiki (covered below), has an RSS feed to notify subscribers of updates to it – in this case, the addition of new reviews. The Public Library of Charlotte and Mecklenburg County have feeds for their events as well as for their 24 branches, each of which has its own web page.[11] Ann Arbor District Library offer feeds in a myriad of formats from their numerous blogs, including by subject list and genre, audience, format, branch and series.[12]

RSS feeds allow the public library to get their information literacy content straight to the user, rather than having to wait for users to come to the library or to the website. It is the best online delivery mechanism available as it takes little effort for either the library or the user to set up.

Wikis

Wikis are not as straightforward or as flexible as blogs and their take-up by public libraries has not been as broad, as a result. However, there are some innovative uses of wikis by public libraries that are worthy of attention.

Foremost is the Book Lovers' Wiki from Princeton Public Library in New Jersey, USA.[13] In the summer of 2006, they set up a wiki for their adult summer reading programme. The aim was to enable participants in the programme to post their own book reviews and comment on other reviews submitted. Unfortunately, at that time the wiki option they chose did not have WYSIWYG (what you see is what you get) functionality, so some HTML coding knowledge was required. This limited the number of people submitting reviews directly onto the wiki; however, reviews e-mailed in by participants were coded by library volunteers so that all reviews were accessible. Since then, WYSIWYG functionality has become standard for wikis, making it easy for anyone to contribute content. Yarra Plenty Regional Libraries[14] in Melbourne, Australia, picked up this idea for their children's summer reading programme and this has since been followed by other public libraries.

St. Joseph County Public Library are using a wiki for their website's information content in the form of subject guides.[15] The guides were created to help users learn about a subject, discover library events and materials and enjoy reading about a hobby/subject of interest. They offer 35 guides in the areas of books, business, information desk, education, entertainment, government, health and fitness, hobbies, local and family history, news and current events and recreation. Although the wiki can only be edited by library staff (and they are easily edited), St. Joseph use the discussion functionality to allow patrons to make a comment, a suggestion for new content, additions or deletions and more. The guides are browseable via the subject guide list and via category and are also fully searchable by keyword.

Wikis are being used prolifically by libraries for staff manuals, including those used for information or reference services, circulation services and troubleshooting. Unfortunately, as they usually reside on staff intranets, we are unable to see them. However, a wiki is an efficient and effective replacement for a paper manual, as it eliminates the need for multiple paper updates. It is also more efficient in that any change to its content will also change the appropriate references within the wiki. It is also more accessible than a paper document, which can only be used by one person at a time, whereas the wiki is only limited by access to a computer.

Wiki software is also being used for a lot of professional development content, such as LISWiki – the Library Science wiki,[16] as an information source, such as the previously mentioned Library Success wiki, and in support of conferences, such as the Computers in Libraries 2007 wiki.[17] Thomas Ford Memorial Library[18] and other smaller libraries have used wiki software for their websites.

Wikis are an effective way of sharing recommended content, as St. Joseph is doing with its subject guides and as Princeton and Yarra Plenty have done with book reviews. Information literacy can come into this not only through the use of the wiki and its content, but also in the sharing of information, from user back to source.

Podcasting

Many public libraries have taken up podcasting with enthusiasm. They have shown that it is as straightforward and easy to use as Web 2.0 tools are in general. Minimal equipment is required, software is freely available for editing, as is the blog software to load it onto, hence making it a podcast, not just an audio download.

There are many events being podcast in public libraries. Princeton Library have podcast their Poetry Readings where poets did public readings of their own poetry at the library.[19] Darien Library have podcasts of their visiting speakers,[20] as do many other public libraries, requiring only the recording and the permission of the speaker to make this possible. They have also tried some interesting things with their podcasts, including one of their first which was an interview with children in the library, asking them who they thought was going to die in the latest Harry Potter book. They also podcast musical performances held in the library and have used interviews with speakers and their presentations as podcasts. The Public Library of Charlotte and Mecklenburg County has teen podcasts with 'news, programs, and commentary created by and for teens'[21] – a notable podcast was their Teen Talk Joke-Off Contest. Content is available through RSS feed and through the iTunes store.

Lansing Public Library in Illinois, USA offer podcasts on how to use their library catalogue and how to set up and use a Yahoo e-mail account, as well as regular podcasts of their adult, teen and technology programmes, all being prime examples of public library information literacy programmes.[223] Denver Public Library has also been podcasting storytimes, but has done so with more recent titles than Darien, with permission from the relevant publishers.[23] Kankakee Public Library in Illinois, USA, offers podcasts, vodcasts and also streaming of selected audio, featuring author talks and guest speakers.[24]

Instant messaging reference

Instant messaging (IM) has been around as a communication medium for quite a few years. However, its usefulness to libraries as a service mechanism has been restricted by the inability of different IM clients to talk to each other. Libraries started offering information services via IM, but were usually restricted to those people using the same IM client as the library. St. Joseph County Public Library[25] and the Public Library of Charlotte and Mecklenburg County[26] are among many libraries that worked around this restriction by having user names for multiple IM clients.

Developments in recent years have made offering this type of service much easier. IM software such as Gaim and Trillian can access multiple IM clients, as can the web-based application Meebo. Many public libraries that used to have multiple software to offer this service have now shifted to using these applications.

With the more recent development of the Meebo widget, libraries can offer IM reference with the help of a widget embedded in a library web page. The advantage of this is that neither the library nor the user needs to have an IM account, as it can all be done through the widget. This opens up the service to a wider range of users and makes it more accessible and easier to use. Darien Library[27] and is an early adopter of this option for IM reference.

Social networking

Public libraries are always looking for ways to reach their users and potential users. The phenomenal growth of social networking websites in the last few years has given public libraries a new frontier to explore.

Flickr and similar photo-sharing websites have been a boon to public libraries, enabling them to show a wider audience the face of the public library. Photos have been posted of library events, presenters, buildings new, old, or being constructed or renovated, library staff and friends, signs and much more. Public libraries become linked to people who have taken photos in or of their buildings and contents. These photos uploaded to Flickr create a network which could not be realized in any other way. Some great examples of public libraries' use of Flickr include Hennepin County Public Library's Ridgedale Teen Art Contest 2007 set;[28] Thomas Ford Memorial Library, which features photos of Ford taken by users around the world;[29] and Darien's New Library set,[30] which includes photos from fundraising and planning as well as the stages of construction.

Public libraries are using Flickr to encourage people to contribute their own photos on particular topics, including local history, photos of the library or surrounding areas and the activities being held there. The National Library in Australia has partnered with Flickr on the Click and Flick[31] project, which allows individuals to post photos to the Picture Australia repository through the National Library's Flickr account. The photographer retains copyright, but the Picture Australia repository has been enriched by the contributions of over 500 people and their 15,000-plus images.

MySpace and Facebook are the social networking sites where people just interact when they are online – a virtual 'Third Place'. As there are millions of people using these sites, public libraries are setting up profiles there so that they are present in this virtual Third Place, as well as in physical space. The Public Library of Charlotte and Mecklenburg County's The Loft (their teen space) has a very successful MySpace profile which has podcasts, blog entries, links to library information including events, and competitions, and has accrued over 1000 friends.[32] Hennepin County Library's MySpace profile even includes a catalogue search box, and has accrued over 900 friends.[33]

YouTube and online video is another aspect of Web 2.0 that libraries are exploring, with multiple aims. Public libraries are using video to promote their services and libraries in general, but also to educate their users. St. Joseph County Public Library produced 'Ray of Light',[34] which shows a 'typical' day in the working life of their staff, and Gail Borden Public Library has a video giving a guided tour of the library.[35] Many public libraries have videos on YouTube about their renovations and new buildings or reading clubs and more than a few have also used YouTube to run video contests for their users, encouraging budding film-makers to share their work on a set theme.

Conclusion

Although not explicitly defined for public libraries, because our audiences are so diverse, public libraries clearly have an information literacy role. How much of that role we take on and in what form is up to each library to decide, within the limits of its own resources. However, Web 2.0 tools make that much easier to do. As libraries utilize these tools for promotional and communication purposes, including teaching information literacy, they position themselves to be able to teach their users about how to utilize those same tools.

There are many more Web 2.0 tools adopted by libraries to reach users both new and potential and to provide services to them more effectively. More tools are emerging on a regular basis. With the advent of these tools, our users' expectations have increased. They expect to be able to hear more from their public library, to communicate with us easily, to learn more about what we offer and to expect that those offerings are straightforward to use. Web 2.0 tools give us the opportunity, at little cost, to do all this and more. You have the chance now to make things happen in your public library's corner of virtual space that will make your community want to come and visit you there too.

References

Lewis, A. (n.d.) *Information Literacy and Public Libraries*, www.informationliteracy.co.uk/Information_literacy/IL_Public_ Libraries.aspx.

Skov, A. (2004) Information Literacy and the Role of Public Libraries, *Scandinavian Public Library Quarterly*, **37** (3), www.splq.info/issues/vol37_3/02.htm.

Resources

1   Ramsay & Reid Scholarships from the State Library of Victoria, www.slv.vic.gov.au/programs/research/scholarships.
2   Connecting Librarian blog, http://connectinglibrarian.blogspot.com.
3   Learning 2.0 from the Public Library of Charlotte & Mecklenburg County, http://plcmcl2-about.blogspot.com.
4   Learning 2.1 from the Public Library of Charlotte & Mecklenburg County, http://explorediscoverplay.blogspot.com.
5   Library Success: a best practices wiki, www.libsuccess.org.
6   Darien Library Blogs, www.darienlibrary.org/blogs.php.

7 Ann Arbor District Library blog-based website, www.aadl.org.

8 Western Springs Historical Society blog, www.westernspringshistory.org.

9 Teen online blog from Eastern Regional Libraries,
   http://teenonlinetor.blogspot.com.

10 Hennepin County Library RSS feeds, www.hclib.org/pub/search/RSS.cfm.

11 RSS feeds from the Public Library of Charlotte & Mecklenburg County,
    http://plcmc.org/programs/rsslist.asp.

12 RSS feeds from Ann Arbor District Library, www.aadl.org/syndication.

13 Princeton Public Library's Book Lovers' Wiki,
    http://booklovers.pbwiki.com/Princeton%20Public%20Library.

14 Yarra Plenty Regional Library's Summer Reading Club wiki,
    http://summerreadingclub.pbwiki.com.

15 Subject guides from St Joseph County Public Library,
    www.libraryforlife.org/subjectguides/index.php/Main_Page.

16 LISWiki – Library and Information Science wiki,
    http://liswiki.org/wiki/Main_Page.

17 Computers in Libraries 2007 wiki, http://cil2007.pbwiki.com.

18 Wiki software used for the website of Thomas Ford Memorial Library,
    www.fordlibrary.org.

19 Poetry readings podcast by Princeton Public Library,
    http://pplpoetpodcast.wordpress.com.

20 Podcasts by Darien Library,
    www.darienlibrary.org/connections/events/archives/podcasts.

21 Library Loft podcasts by the Public Library of Charlotte & Mecklenburg
    County, www.libraryloft.org/podcasts.asp.

22 Podcasts from Lansing Public Library, www.lansing.lib.il.us/podcasts.html.

23 'Stories for kids' podcasts from Denver Public Library,
    http://podcast.denverlibrary.org.

24 Podcasts from Kankakee Public Library,
    www.kankakee.lib.il.us/Podcasts.html.

25 'IM a Librarian!' from St. Joseph County Public Library,
    www.sjcpl.org/asksjcpl/asksjcpl.html.

26 'Ask a Librarian' from the Public Library of Charlotte & Mecklenburg
    County,
    http://plcmc.org/Online/Ask_a_Librarian/default.asp.

27 'Have a question?' from Darien Library,
    www.darienlibrary.org/contact.php.

28 'Ridgedale Teen Art Contest 2007' Flickr set from Hennepin County Public
    Library,
    www.flickr.com/photos/hennepincountylibrary/sets/72157601196619180.

29 'Thommy Ford' Flickr set from Thomas Ford Memorial Library,
    www.flickr.com/photos/thomasfordmemoriallibrary.

30 'New Library' Flickr set from Darien Library,
    www.flickr.com/photos/darienlibrary/collections/72157600607391824.

31 'Click a flick' Picture Australia/Yahoo collaboration using Flickr,
    www.nla.gov.au/pub/gateways/issues/80/story01.html.

32 'The Loft @ Imaginon' profile, www.myspace.com/libraryloft.

33 'Hennepin County Library' profile,
    www.myspace.com/hennepincountylibrary.

34 'Ray of Light', St. Joseph County Public Library Version on YouTube,
    www.youtube.com/watch?v=vrtYdFV_Eak.

35 'Quick tour of the Gail Borden Public Library' on YouTube,
    www.youtube.com/watch?v=_RezCELJJc4.

Part 3
Library 2.0 and IL in practice

Chapter 6

Engage or enrage: the blog as an assessment tool

GEORGINA PAYNE

In November 2006, 66 students at the University of Northampton, UK, embarked on an information blog assessment, created by library staff to teach information skills. This chapter is the story behind the assessment: the assessment brief, the reactions of students, the impact on tutors and our various successes and failings as we journeyed towards the final deadline day of 7 May 2007.

The assessment brief

A significant feature of the information blog was its integration as a summative assessment into a first-year information skills module offered by the University's business school. The module curriculum was delivered by academic librarians and business school academics. It included 13 weeks of lectures and seminars dedicated to topics such as censorship, web usability, information management, search strategies, evaluating information, Web 2.0, and the information society. Using Blogger (www.blogger.com), the students were asked to write a minimum of ten blog posts of around 250 words reflecting upon the range, quality, reliability, effectiveness, delivery and organization of the information they encountered on a daily basis. They were instructed that their blogs should be evaluative and analytical. From 20 November 2006 to 7 January 2007 the students were given the chance to experiment with their blogs and tutors gave formative feedback, while the summative period ran from 8 January 2007 to midnight on 7 May 2007. It was stipulated that the students should spread their posts out evenly across the summative period, rather than writing all their entries at the eleventh hour. The choice of post topic was deliberately left open to allow the students the freedom to blog on issues within their information environment that really mattered to them, as is the nature of true blogging. They were also given advice on blog style and etiquette, privacy issues and topic ideas. The information blog assessment formed 50% of the students' module marks, which we hoped would sufficiently motivate the students to post regularly and work hard on their blogs, and it was administered and marked by the academic librarians.

So, why did we choose a blog? We thought the blog online diary format offered specific pedagogic benefits:

1 The possibility of engaging students in an assessment over a sustained period of time, linking week-by-week to the curriculum, potentially countering strategic and surface learning.
2 The blog afforded creative opportunities, allowing students to become information creators and contributors, gaining a sense of their own agency in the production of information.

As Jean Burgess comments in Blogging to Learn, Learning to Blog (2006, 106):

> These uses of blogging contribute to a reconceptualization of students as critical, collaborative, and creative participants in the social construction of knowledge and are compatible with the social constructionist framework for learning, which – unlike the 'transmission of knowledge' model, assumes that students must become active partners in the construction of knowledge with their peers, academic staff and the wider social context of the disciplines in which they work.

It was to further this sense of the students' own participation in the construction of knowledge that we decided not to use the blogging software within our VLE, but instead we chose Blogger, which would give the students an authentic blogging experience. We also enabled them to develop their own blog persona by allowing the students to customize the look and feel of their blogs and by letting them choose their own blog title, login, web address, and display name.

So, how would it all work in practice? Even before beginning the assessment, questions immediately surfaced. Would the students post regularly? How would students cope with the Blogger software? How would students feel about posting into the blogosphere? To evaluate student and tutor response as the assessment progressed we used five research instruments:

1   Pre-assessment questionnaire to gauge the students' initial response.
2   Semi-structured interviews undertaken with a sample of students while the information blog assessment was in process.
3   Observation of student posting behaviour undertaken via RSS web feeds.
4   Observation of student and tutor behaviour undertaken via correspondence and discussions between students and tutors.
5   Post-assessment questionnaire to gauge the students' final response.

Student response

The 66 student bloggers were mostly management and business students studying courses provided by the Northampton Business School, but the module was an elective and some of the students were drawn from other disciplines. Approaching 90% of the students were in the 18 to 21 age bracket and there were 30 women and 36 men. Most of the students were excited on hearing about the assignment and upon setting up their personalized blogs. Comments from the pre-assessment questionnaire included:

> I feel that it is something well different compared to any other assignments. It is a great way to express what you are thinking and can share it with other people online.

and

> I feel this will certainly be an interesting assessment. A very unique way to assess on how students can process, assess and produce information for a wide audience. Very good idea though! Should be very interesting!

Out of the 66 students, there were only four negative comments in the pre-assessment questionnaire. These comments included a fear of posting publicly online, a know-it-all attitude and concerns that the information blog assessment was a pilot. Towards the end of the assessment another questionnaire was administered which elicited a similarly positive response.

Posting behaviour: strategy and deviance

From mid-December we began monitoring the students' blogging behaviour using RSS feeds. Whenever a student posted, an alert was sent to the tutor and the date of the post was recorded. In total, the students posted 529 entries. Figure 6.1 shows their collective posting behaviour. Strategic learning was in evidence from the outset, with only 20 students posting during the formative period. The beginning of the summative period saw an initial boost in the number of posts, but this enthusiasm waned until a final surge in the week before the 7 May deadline, when around 40% of students wrote all their posts. The students knew their final mark would be linked to the regularity of their posts. If all posts were submitted in the last week they were told their grade would be capped at D-. Despite repeated warnings from tutors, a large number of students could not handle the small yet regular effort that was required for the information blog or were wilfully oblivious to the necessity of regular posting.

However, the aberrant posting behaviour was not all down to the students. For ten weeks in the middle of the 17-week summative period, the module curriculum was taught by business school staff, rather than by

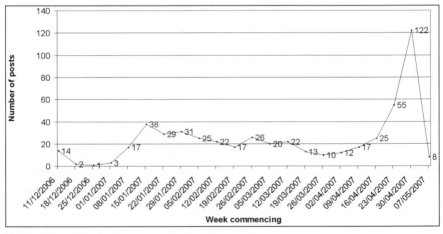

Figure 6.1   Student posting behaviour pattern

the librarians administering the assessment. Posting frequency may have declined due to reduced librarian–student contact.

By 26 March 2007 it was possible to identify four distinct posting behaviours:

1   Super posters: Eight students (12%), two men and six women, who posted more than the necessary 10 posts comfortably within the summative period. These students were enthusiastic and engaged with the assessment.
2   Strategists: 16 students (24%), nine men and seven women, who posted exactly 10 posts comfortably within the time period. Again, most of these students were enthusiastic and engaged with the assessment.
3   Amber gamblers: 16 students (24%), nine men and seven women, who had just enough weeks left until the deadline to spread out their posts.
4   Red light jumpers: 26 students (40%), 16 men and 10 women, who did not have enough weeks left to spread out their posts.

So, although some students grappled with regular posting, 60% of the students got to grips with the concept, with many students commenting positively about the posting timescale in the post-assessment questionnaire:

> It is hard to keep doing it, but it is good for us. It means we can keep learning every week.

and

> This is a suitable timescale. I tried to post a blog every other week and it became a routine that was easy to follow.

There were also three students who exhibited deviant posting behaviour! One student created gobbledygook posts as placeholders, with the intention of going back and writing proper posts later. Another student found the facility in Blogger that enabled her to fake her posting dates. Another student exploited a loophole in the assessment brief and wrote headings for each post, completing each post just before the 7 May deadline. All these behaviours were picked up by the use of RSS feeds.

Technical issues and digital natives

The use of Blogger and the ongoing observation via RSS feeds did not come without a price. In giving the students the freedom to choose their own Blogger login and web address we opened ourselves up to an avalanche of technical support issues. Nearly one-third of the students forgot their login and had difficulties using the Blogger forgotten password retrieval facility and, despite training, some also struggled to create new posts, insert images and view their blog. Most of these students were aged 18 to 21, part of the 'digital native' generation. Although the Blogger software seemed intuitive to the thirty-something and forty-something academic librarians, this was not the case for the students. They stumbled over basic technical issues and while they may have been born into a digital world, not all were born digital. As well as troubleshooting technical problems, using RSS feeds to monitor and record the student posts week by week was also labour intensive. Posting patterns and deviant posting behaviour were detected, but at the cost of tutor sanity.

Post quality

A significant number of students latched onto topical news items, e.g. the Shilpa Shetty Big Brother incident, and simply described how they felt about the subject matter rather than examining the information in terms of its reliability and accuracy, organization and structure, usability or cultural significance. To resolve the problem, tutors provided individual feedback, even during the summative period. Most students amended their posts accordingly, but the reasons certain students failed to attain higher levels of analysis formed an ongoing debate among tutors. It was argued that the assessment was too abstract and that we were asking too much of first-year students, who should perhaps be expected to demonstrate skills associated with the lower zones of Bloom's taxonomy (1964), knowledge, understanding and application, as opposed to the upper zones, analysis, synthesis and evaluation. Was it that the information blog assessment expected too much in terms of confidence, maturity and the ability to think outside the box? We don't think so. Of the seven students who received A grades, six were in the 18 to 21 bracket, demonstrating it was possible for them to achieve this level of analysis.

In addition, the overall quality of the students' blogs spread the gamut, with 25% of students receiving B- or above. The grades of those students who wrote their posts immediately prior to the deadline were capped a D-, somewhat skewing the grade distribution, but the distribution would otherwise have clustered around the C- to C+ range, indicating that students struggled more with posting regularly than they did with analysis and evaluation.

In terms of final grade, there was no correlation with major subject, age or gender. Nor was the assessment skewed in favour of those who enjoyed writing and posting. Although the super posters were predominantly female, their enthusiasm for excess posting did not translate into a higher grade. The modal grade for both super posters and strategists was A-, while the median grades were C and C-, respectively. One of the super posters, with a total of 18 posts, persistently posted off-topic and failed the assessment. Asking the students to evaluate and analyse information as *information* required them to utilize generic higher-level thinking skills. Students of all backgrounds could be found at each level of the grade distribution, indicating the assessment was equitable, realistic and achievable for first-year students.

Posting into the blogosphere

In the post-assessment questionnaire and the semi-structured interviews, we asked the students to express how they felt about posting live into the blogosphere. Some students commented upon the freedom and the creative and communicative possibilities, while others expressed their fears:

> It feels good that you are free to write your own things on the web.

> It's something really interesting because you can put pictures, videos, text – you can create something yourself and other people have got the chance to login, read what you've written about and put some comments, so there is the possibility to discuss something with other people. I think it's quite exciting.

> I hate the thought.

> Uncertain, because one of my posts had a comment posted that wasn't very nice.

In the post-assessment questionnaire we also asked the students whom they would like to be able to view their blog. More than half wanted their blog live in the blogosphere, but around 44% wanted their blog to be hidden behind the University's firewall, while a couple of students wanted their blog to be for the tutor's eyes only. The reasons articulated included a lack of confidence about their blog content or anxiety about who could read their blog and the response it might elicit. For the tutors there were also possible public relations issues. While many students produced excellent blogs, a couple of the poorer blogs included ill-considered extremist comments or grammatical and typographical errors. While the students' blogs were not branded with the University's details, some revealed it was for a university assignment. Did the University really want this out in the public domain? Many students have incriminating MySpace or Facebook accounts, but, significantly, these are not created under the auspices of the University.

What next?

Next year the information blog assessment will run again. The assessment proved to be equitable and fulfilled most of our pedagogic objectives. The students gained a theoretical understanding of their information environment from the curriculum, which they reflected upon with respect to their personal information environment and then created and published their own thoughts and analysis. Most students demonstrated an increased information awareness, enjoyed the creative opportunity and achieved greater or lesser degrees of analysis and evaluation. The weaknesses of the information blog were its technical support demands, the link between the student's final grade and posting regularity, student anxieties and public relations issues derived from posting to the blogosphere and the ten-week curriculum break when the students were out of face-to-face contact with the librarians administering the assessment. Next year there will be some changes. At the expense of blogging authenticity, but to minimize technical support, we have decided to use the University's in-house blogging software, located within our VLE. This should also eliminate any public relations issues and reduce student anxieties about who may read their blogs. To keep the spirit of blogging alive, the students will still be able to experiment creatively with their blogs and they will be able to read and comment on each other's blogs. The academic librarian component of the curriculum is also to be delivered in an unbroken teaching block, to enable consistent student–tutor contact during the information blog assessment period. Finally, rather than fighting the students' proclivity to work to deadlines, there will be no penalty attached to posting all entries in the final week, but these students will miss out on the opportunity for formative feedback, which could significantly improve their grade.

References

Bloom, B., Krathwohl, D. and Masia, B. (1964) *Taxonomy of Educational Objectives: the classification of educational goals. Handbook 2: affective domain,* Longman.

Burgess, J. (2006) Blogging to Learn, Learning to Blog. In Bruns, A. and Jacobs, J. (eds), *Uses of Blogs,* Peter Lang.

Chapter 7

Using Wikipedia to eavesdrop on the scholarly conversation

ANNE-MARIE DEITERING

Every few months on the information literacy discussion list ILI-L someone will raise the question 'how can I convince students not to use Wikipedia?' At Oregon State University, we do the opposite. We require every one of our first-year composition students to use Wikipedia as a background source for a researched argument essay. In the last two years, activities using the collaboratively authored encyclopedia have become a cornerstone of our information literacy curriculum.

The challenge

In 2001, the Oregon State University (OSU) Libraries partnered with writing faculty to deliver information literacy instruction in every section of WR 121, OSU's First Year Composition (FYC) course. As the only course all OSU undergraduates are required to take, a major goal of FYC is to introduce students to the processes and practice of academic writing. When the libraries came on board our challenge became: how do we help FYC students learn to research like scholars?

OSU instruction librarians use the metaphor of a scholarly conversation to describe the process of academic research. Davidson and Crateau introduced this metaphor in 1998, after developing the idea for four years in OSU's Honors Writing Course. The conversation metaphor emphasizes broad, open-minded exploration. Just as someone (with social skills) will spend some time listening before jumping into a conversation with new people, someone with information literacy skills will 'eavesdrop' on the scholarly conversation taking place in the literature before developing and announcing their own thesis.

The 'eavesdropping' part of scholarly research is difficult to teach. In the early stages of our collaboration, librarians and writing faculty alike reported that too many students were developing their arguments first and doing their research later. For these students, 'research' meant 'find quotations that support my thesis'. They were not learning from the sources they found; they were not discovering new ideas or lines of enquiry. In short, they were not researching like scholars.

To be successful we needed to do more than show students new databases and skills; to research like scholars they needed a new way of thinking about the nature of knowledge itself. To see this, it is helpful to look at the work of Ernest Pascarella and Patrick Terenzini (2005). In *How College Affects Students*, they review the huge body of research examining the cognitive, social and other skills students develop as a result of higher education. Their work serves as a good reminder that most of our students come to us understanding knowledge as something that is revealed – by teachers, by books, by parents. If knowledge is revealed, then research is simply a process of finding the perfect source that reveals the truth about an unfamiliar topic, or that supports a truth they already accept.

To research like scholars, students need to see knowledge as something that is constructed. This means accepting the idea that some problems defy simple answers (Pascarella and Terenzini, 2005). Part of researching like a scholar is developing a tolerance for ambiguity and an ability to develop an argument when the 'right' answer is not obvious. In this framework, research becomes the process of gathering new ideas, or building blocks, and using those to construct new meaning. The first step in this kind of research process is open-minded, reflective exploration.

What we do

Davidson and Crateau (1998) argue that most instruction librarians are not used to teaching an exploratory research process. They point out that research instruction usually focuses on helping students narrow and focus their topics and queries. Marchionini (2006) adds a useful dimension to this, suggesting that it is not only our teaching but also our tools that emphasize focused queries. He identifies three types of search: lookup, learning and investigation.

Lookup searching is the most basic of these activities, and the easiest to do in search engines and library databases. To do it successfully, the user needs to use the 'analytical search strategies' and 'carefully specified queries' taught in many library instruction sessions (Marchionini, 2006, 42). For learning and investigation, the learner needs to go beyond lookup to exploratory search. Where a lookup search focuses on eliminating the irrelevant, an exploratory search focuses on retrieving the potentially relevant, providing a rich pool of knowledge for the learner to browse.

Our first attempt at creating an assignment that would help students explore illustrates the limitations of library instruction and search tools that focus the query too quickly. In 2004 we replaced one of the library instruction sessions in FYC with a series of five linked assignments the students completed independently during the early stages of the research process. Broad exploration was encouraged most directly in Assignment 2, which asked students to familiarize themselves with a variety of perspectives on their topics, and to take note of important speakers, concepts and vocabulary.

In our first attempt to meet these objectives we sent the students to search engines and multidisciplinary databases, and asked them to browse titles, abstracts and other metadata. This approach failed. Students who chose to argue topics about which they already had strong opinions had difficulty finding alternative points of view amid the mass of results they retrieved. Students who chose to argue unfamiliar topics were not any better off. They simply did not know enough about their subjects to generate useful search terms, or to effectively evaluate those resources they did find. In short, most of our students could not use these tools to do an exploratory search. They did not have enough knowledge about their topics, or about scholarly processes, to find a rich browsing experience in their results lists.

We believed that our students would have an easier time exploring their topics using traditional reference sources. Encyclopedia articles or review articles would address students' subject knowledge gaps and would also address their process knowledge gaps, by suggesting additional lines of enquiry. With that in mind, we set out to redesign Assignment 2. At that time, we had a licence for a general online encyclopedia that was not getting much use. We also noticed that our students were increasingly finding

Wikipedia pages in search engines, and talking to them made it clear that most of them had no idea what a wiki was. We decided to create an assignment that sent students both to our proprietary reference sources and to Wikipedia.

Wikipedia

We immediately ran into trouble with this plan. Using topics and keywords from previous terms' assignments in our online encyclopedia, sample search after sample search failed. Sometimes better keywords might have solved the problem, but the thought of trying to help students generate more effective keywords in an unmediated, online assignment was daunting. Even more worrying, those searches that did result in articles were scarcely better. The articles themselves were awkwardly formatted for the online environment, difficult to navigate and did not provide much in the way of hyperlinks or additional resources.

In Wikipedia, these sample searches reliably produced results. The articles retrieved were easy to navigate. Extensive hyperlinking and lists of related resources made further exploration easy and fun. We realized that while these tools were both online encyclopedias, they delivered profoundly different user experiences.

The content in Wikipedia is not organized in a formal hierarchy or taxonomy, but it is organized. Ideas and topics are connected to each other using the flattened, hyperlinked structure of Web 2.0. This is what creates the rich browsing experience that makes it an ideal resource for broad exploration. At the same time, Wikipedia's content is user-generated. Our students tend to pick current topics for their argument papers, and those topics will be integrated into a Web 2.0 encyclopedia much faster than they will be in a resource produced by traditional scholarly processes. Similarly, Wikipedia's digital nature means that any topic of interest to any group of people, no matter how small, can be added to the resource.

In short, the dynamic social environment of the read/write web was so much better for broad exploration than that provided by traditional reference sources that we came to believe that if we asked students to compare these tools side by side we would only convince them that library research tools were not worth the bother. We decided to focus the exploration assignment on Wikipedia alone.

Knowledge creation

While ease of use was the first reason we decided to use Wikipedia as an information literacy tool, an additional benefit emerged very quickly. One of the goals of the FYC programme is to introduce students to the processes and practice of academic writing. The goal of academic writing, in short, is knowledge creation. As mentioned above, the idea that knowledge is something that can be created is, by itself, a new concept for many of our students.

Scholarly books and journals are not transparent. Where those who have experience with scholarly communication can recognize the clues obvious in a works cited list or literature review, a neophyte has difficulty seeing the point. A term like 'peer reviewed' or 'refereed' suggests a host of things to the scholar, but to the first-year student the requirement to find 'five peer-reviewed articles' might as well be written in another language. It is difficult for students to see the knowledge contained in these sources as constructed because they cannot see how that construction happened.

Wikipedia and other scholarly Web 2.0 tools make the construction process so transparent that a beginner can easily follow it. It is undoubtedly true that this transparency is precisely what makes many scholars sceptical of Web 2.0 tools. With guidance, however, it provides us with an opportunity to help students understand the bigger picture of knowledge creation.

A standard component of wiki software is versioning, or the ability to see (and if necessary revert to) prior versions of content. For the student, these history pages provide an easy way to trace the discourse about a topic within an online community. In Assignment 2 of the Information Literacy Portfolio (ILP), we require all students to identify an article (or articles) about their topic on Wikipedia, and to visit the history pages for their articles. After visiting the history pages they must analyse the page's changes over time and reflect on how they will use the page in their own argument.

Versioning is standard in most wikis, but the requirement that all articles be written from a neutral point of view (NPOV) is a distinctive part of Wikipedia's culture. The NPOV requirement is one of three content requirements for Wikipedia and, as founder Jimmy Wales says, it is 'absolute and non-negotiable' (http://en.wikipedia.org/wiki/Npov). When students examine their history pages, therefore, they are seeing a particular type of knowledge construction. They do not see advocates developing arguments in support of one position or another. Instead, where the system works, they see a community of people attempting to represent all of the significant points of view about a topic in a neutral way. While this can be seen on the main article pages, it is even clearer on the discussion pages for each article. We require students to examine and analyse these discussion pages for their articles.

For our purposes, Wikipedia gives our students a front-row view of knowledge creation in action. In addition, the points of view represented in the articles, and in the discussion pages, are themselves the building blocks with which our students can start to define their own voice within the scholarly conversation.

Conclusion

A key component of our success, therefore, is close collaboration with the writing faculty. In the last year, they have added a requirement to the argument essay that pushes the students to find four 'background' sources and four 'speaker' sources to use as support for their arguments. This distinction helps students understand the rhetorical difference between their Wikipedia articles, and the ideas and perspectives they can mine from within those articles. As librarians, we can talk about the value of sources in a variety of ways, but the impact of this lesson is much stronger when it comes from both librarians and classroom faculty.

At the same time, this assignment poses some challenges. Many faculty members and graduate teaching assistants (GTAs) are sceptical about Wikipedia's value as a source of any kind, and choose to ban it entirely instead of helping students use it appropriately. When they hear that we send all OSU students to this resource deliberately, it can make them sceptical of our programme as a whole. Very occasionally, we even get negative feedback from students who do not believe they should be asked to consult this potentially unreliable source for any reason. On the other hand, articulating our reasons for including Wikipedia in our information literacy curriculum has sparked some useful and meaningful conversations with students and faculty about Web 2.0 and student learning.

The biggest challenge, of course, is making the assignment meaningful and useful for as many students as possible. Because the assignment is given to students before they meet the librarian, or receive any face-to-face instruction, some students do not see the larger purpose behind the ILP. While we explain the objectives and rationale clearly in each section of the ILP, it is not surprising that some students skip that explanation and go right to the step-by-step instructions to get through the assignment as quickly as possible. By focusing on the individual tasks, these students may fail to see the value of the research process the ILP introduces.

There will always be students who do not engage with this assignment. Those students, at a minimum, learn a little more about Wikipedia, a tool they are probably using anyway. At the same time, it is not uncommon to hear students say things like 'I spent an hour and a half last night reading Wikipedia.' While the content of that reading is undoubtedly not entirely scholarly, it is impossible to imagine a college student ten years ago saying 'Dude, I spent an hour last night reading the encyclopedia.' This aspect of the dynamic web, that it makes exploration and discovery easy and fun, is very exciting as we think about ways to use the read/write web as a tool for scholarly enquiry and information literacy.

References

Davidson, J. R. and Crateau, C. A. (1998) Intersections: teaching research through a rhetorical lens, *Research Strategies*, **16** (4), 245-57.

Marchionini, G. (2006) Exploratory Search: from finding to understanding, *Communications of the ACM*, **49** (4), 41-6.

Pascarella, E. T. and Terenzini, P. T. (2005) *How College Affects Students: a third decade of research*, Vol. 2, Jossey-Bass.

Chapter 8

Information literacy and RSS feeds at LSE

CHRISTOPHER FRYER and JANE SECKER

Introduction

This chapter describes how RSS has been used at the London School of Economic and Political Science (LSE) to enhance access to information on training courses, including information literacy classes, for staff and students. RSS underpins much of what we recognize as Web 2.0 and social software. In his recent book, Bradley (2007) argues that in order to fully exploit social software in libraries, it is essential to understand RSS technology. Even a basic understanding can allow all librarians, not just those running a schedule of teaching or training, to make their information more accessible. However, our experiences show that RSS has information literacy implications: users must re-think how they access information on the web. Rather than visiting a website to see what is new, users are afforded a mechanism for picking up new information automatically. The tools required, while simple to use, arguably do require a greater level of information literacy on the part of users. Therefore, paradoxically, while RSS has provided LSE with an opportunity to make training information more widely available, staff and students need greater information literacy skills to fully exploit the technology.

What is RSS?

There is still some disagreement over what RSS actually stands for. Originally, it meant 'RDF Site Summary' (where RDF is the Resource Description

Framework, www.w3.org/RDF), but it is now generally agreed to stand for 'Really Simple Syndication'. Each definition provides an insight into its potential uses: as a 'summary' of what's new or has recently changed on a website; or as a method for 'syndication' of content, allowing information to be re-used in a variety of contexts.

RSS is a dialect of XML. It is a machine-readable language, much like HTML, designed to provide a rigid framework in which information can be contained. At its simplest, an RSS document provides a set of *items*, each of which has a *title*, a *description* and a *link* to an online resource. A series of *items*, almost always provided in some kind of chronological order, makes up a *feed*. The feed itself contains additional metadata indicating, for example, the source (e.g. the website) from which the items were drawn, the time and date of its publication, and the contact details of the publisher.

Since a feed is broken down into individual items, it follows that the medium is really only suitable for publishing quantized information. This explains its rapid uptake within the news media: each item corresponds to a discrete news story. In this example, the headline becomes the title, a short summary of the story becomes the description, and the link is a URL pointing to the full version of the story.

Similarly, blogs provide an RSS feed, each item corresponding to an individual post. But a link need not point to a web page: a 'podcast', for example, is simply a series of audio files whose URLs have been published in an RSS document.

From a user perspective, the strength of RSS lies in two additional pieces of information contained within a feed: its publication date, and its *time-to-live*, i.e. the period of time a given copy of the feed remains valid. This allows the user to subscribe to the feed using an RSS-reading tool (such as the web-based tools Google Reader or Bloglines), which, when the document expires, will check to see if there is a newer copy available, and if so, to present it to the user without his or her intervention. A user who previously visited a large number of online resources to see what, if anything, had changed now need only open their RSS reader of choice and immediately find new items of interest.

There are online services that provide RSS-reading capabilities, such as Ask.com's Bloglines (www.bloglines.com) and iGoogle (www.google.com/ig), a personalized home page service offered by the search provider. Additionally, there are stand-alone RSS readers that can be installed on your PC and do not use a web browser; others are provided for mobile devices such as hand-held computers and mobile phones. For those less familiar with what RSS is, the BBC provides a useful overview of this technology on its website (http://news.bbc.co.uk/1/hi/help/3223484.stm). Sauers (2006) also provides an in-depth look at RSS in his book on blogging and RSS for librarians.

Training at LSE: the problems

LSE has a number of training providers in different departments throughout the School. These include: the Library, IT Training, the Centre for Learning Technology (CLT) and the Teaching and Learning Centre. Each maintains its own website which lists the upcoming training sessions they offer. However, staff and students had, until recently, no way of knowing which department provided specific courses without visiting each website individually. Past discussions aimed at resolving this problem had focused on providing one, centrally managed website listing all upcoming courses, and an online booking system for all. However, departments had invested time and resources in their own databases and booking systems, each tailored to their specific requirements, and were reluctant to invest in the development of a new system.

Despite their differences in implementation, all LSE's training providers' websites share obvious similarities: they publish information about individual training sessions according to a schedule, and provide a mechanism to book online. RSS presents itself as an obvious format in which to republish the information, since each training session corresponds nicely to an RSS item. If all providers were to publish an RSS feed of their upcoming sessions, we could re-use the data in a number of ways:

- embed the feeds in websites, including the institutional portal, LSEForYou, to allow content to be displayed dynamically
- embed the feeds in the institutional Virtual Learning Environment, Moodle
- display the contents of feeds on plasma screens around the campus
- combine the feeds into a single, central web page linking to the appropriate booking system.

Over time, as awareness of RSS grows, we hope staff and students might choose to subscribe to the training feed. Regardless, we are able to provide the same information in multiple online locations.

How we used RSS feeds at LSE

The RSS 2.0 namespace – the convention describing what kinds of data may be included in a feed – only allows for a limited number of elements. However, since RSS is a subset of XML, it is extensible by referring to additional namespaces. In addition to the title and description fields, our implementation requires a way to indicate the date and time of a training session, its location, the department or individual who is running the session, and the audience for which it is intended (e.g. staff or postgraduate students). By referring to two additional namespaces in our RSS documents – the RSS Events module, and the Dublin Core Terms namespace – we are able to provide this information while ensuring the document remains valid XML. This is important, since much RSS-reading software will refuse to display invalid XML.

Every day, each training provider runs an automated program that generates an RSS feed by querying their course database. Another program collects all these RSS feeds and aggregates the information for display on a single page (Figure 8.1). The inclusion of scheduling information allows

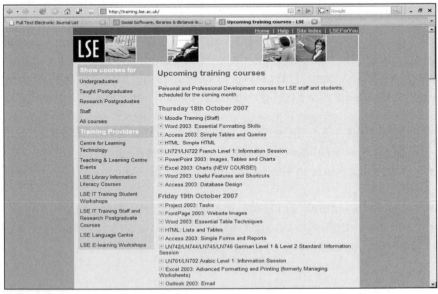

Figure 8.1   The LSE Training Portal, http://training.lse.ac.uk.

Reproduced with thanks by permission of the London School of Economics.

this page to display the sessions in chronological order, and the *audience* metadata allows users to filter the list for courses tailored to their requirements. (We agreed a controlled vocabulary for the audience metadata. See http://training.lse.ac.uk/docs for more information.) Users no longer need to know in advance who is offering a particular course, since each item on the page contains a link to the organizing department's booking system.

In addition, the aggregating program generates new RSS feeds for specific audiences. The student feed can then be displayed in the School's institutional VLE, Moodle, which is equipped to handle RSS. The institutional portal, meanwhile, recognizes a user's status – e.g. staff or student – and provides information and tasks appropriate to that role. This now includes our training feeds.

Finally, LSE has installed a number of large plasma screens around the campus, displaying room bookings, computer workstation availability and public lectures. We decided to take advantage of their presence by providing our training schedule, formatted in large type for display on these screens. In this way, passing staff and students might notice an interesting course, and visit the training portal for more information.

Other ways LSE uses RSS technology

The Centre for Learning Technology is also using RSS technology to feed news content onto its website. The Centre maintains a blog where all CLT staff can post information they wish to share with their colleagues or anyone interested in learning technology more generally. However, blog postings that are particularly newsworthy can be designated as 'CLTNews' which means they automatically appear on the CLT home page in the news section on the right of the screen. Figure 8.2 on page 100 shows how this news information appears on the CLT home page. Posting news to a blog, but also having the content appear on the website, saves time and effort and helps ensure the website looks up to date.

Other libraries using RSS feeds

In the United States a number of libraries are using RSS feeds to make their information more accessible. For example, MIT Libraries (http://libraries.mit. edu/help/rss/barton) use RSS to publish information about new books being added to the library catalogue. Feeds are published in numerous subject areas and this can be added to a feed reader or incorporated into any web

Figure 8.2   The News content on the CLT website comes directly from
the CLT Blog, http://clt.lse.ac.uk.

Reproduced with thanks by permission of the Centre for Learning
Technology, London School of Economics.

page. This functionality could be particularly useful for an academic
department, allowing them to add the feed to their own web pages or directly
into courses in a virtual learning environment. MIT Libraries also have a
general library news feed and a feed for new theses added to their repository.
They also maintain a useful link of RSS feeds for research, which includes
information about which publishers offer RSS feeds. For details of this page
see http://libraries.mit.edu/help/rss/feeds.html.

Meanwhile, Amazon also provides RSS feeds for new books on a huge
variety of subjects, which can also be used in a variety of different ways. More
details about the Amazon feeds are available at: www.amazon.com/gp/
tagging/rss-help.html. Increasingly publishers and library databases are also
adding RSS functionality to enable users to set up feeds for searches they
may wish to run frequently. For example, EBSCO and Web of Science
recently added RSS feeds to their databases, so in place of having search
results sent by e-mail, users could set up a feed to have searched results
pushed to them. Once again Sauers (2006) is a valuable source of
information about how libraries and other organizations are using feeds,
with Chapter 8 looking specifically at how you might create feeds yourself.

The future at LSE

At LSE RSS technology has provided an ideal solution, bringing disparate training information from four providers together in one site, the Training Portal (http://training.lse.ac.uk). Users visiting the site can filter courses to display those suitable for staff, or those for students. The team planned a formal launch with students at Freshers' Fair in autumn 2007, developing a logo and promotional giveaways with the web address prominently displayed. The site was promoted beforehand to staff through the weekly internal e-mail newsletter. The team recently invited several other LSE training providers to join the initiative, including the Staff Development Unit, the Language Centre and the Careers Service, and have been exploring whether their courses can be included. The intention is that in the future all non-academic course information could be accessible through the Training Portal.

The other key advantage of using RSS to power the Training Portal is the ability to incorporate a link to the site and the feed into other websites. So, for example, the RSS feed has been added to Moodle and the institutional portal. All the training providers still maintain their own websites with details of their own courses and a booking system, but both IT Training and the Library website have a scrolling link to the feed displaying other courses running in the next week. Eventually, if our users are using feed readers and fully understand RSS they may wish to subscribe to the feed so they can be updated automatically.

Conclusion

As Bradley (2007) and Sauers (2006) recognize, RSS, despite its relative simplicity, is an enormously powerful technology which changes the way information is made available on the web. It also allows information to be presented in a variety of different ways for different audiences.

RSS, as well as providing a valuable solution to enhancing training provision at LSE, is arguably another tool, along with search engines, that can be hugely valuable to those with well developed information literacy skills. In autumn 2006 LSE offered a new course for staff that focused on finding and reading blogs and using an RSS reader. The course was taught by staff in the Centre for Learning Technology and explaining clearly how RSS works was a key task for the trainers. Unsurprisingly, grappling with this new way of reading the web was challenging for many attending the course. From autumn 2007 library staff and learning technologists are working together to develop a new course for PhD students and researchers on utilizing RSS to keep up to date. This course is partly as a reaction to the increasing number of publishers and library systems that have added RSS functionality to their databases. Librarians and trainers elsewhere may also find themselves having to teach users about RSS, and how to identify and use feeds. It is difficult to predict how RSS technologies will develop; for some researchers already, checking their feed reader can be as important as checking their e-mail account. In fact, it is even possible to check your e-mail using RSS technology. However, as technology develops it is clear that teaching people to navigate the web and find information is a skill that constantly needs updating to take into account new tools and technologies. RSS is currently an important tool that trainers can use, but one which requires support if our users are to exploit it fully.

References

Bradley, P. (2007) *How to Use Web 2.0 in Your Library*, Facet Publishing.
Sauers, M. P. (2006) *Blogging and RSS: a librarian's guide*, Information Today.

Chapter 9

Library instruction on the go: podcasting at the Kresge Library

JENNIFER ZIMMER and SALLY ZIPH

Introduction

The Kresge Business Administration Library serves a population of 3500 business school students plus faculty and staff of the Ross School of Business at the University of Michigan. Like most libraries, the Kresge Library had a set of traditional, classroom-based, library instruction sessions designed to introduce the students to the overwhelming amount of resources available to them at the Library. In recent years, the Library had reduced the number of traditional classroom-based instruction programmes in order to try web-based methods, such as posting instruction session handouts on the website and 'Camtasia' type videos with screen-shots that would allow students to get the information when and where they needed it.

Podcasting seemed to be the next logical step in this process as it allowed the Library to provide fairly detailed instruction in a preferred format that was portable and could be listened to anywhere at any time. Podcasts also allowed for the incorporation of images, links, and if desired, video, all of which could be used to provide interaction for the users with the information that was being discussed. In addition, the chaptering features of the podcasts allowed users to listen to just the parts of the podcast that were important to them at the moment, allowing for a more personalized instruction session and saving the user time. The students could also listen to the podcasts as many times as needed, supporting those who are auditory learners and those who find repetition beneficial. Lastly, the medium allowed users to listen and learn wherever it was convenient for them. They did not have to be in a classroom at a particular time in order to learn about the Library and its resources.

The Library began a pilot podcasting project in the summer of 2006 based in part on the successes experienced at the University of Michigan Dental School. While several methods were explored for creating the podcasts, it was decided that the best way to create podcasts quickly and easily was to purchase the right equipment. The desired functionality of an 'enhanced' podcast with images to support the narrative, chaptering and linking capabilities could quickly and seamlessly be produced in a Mac environment. Based on recommendations from the Apple representative, the Library purchased a 15 in. MacBook Pro with OSX (version 10.4.5), 1.83 GHz Intel Core Duo, and 512 Mb DDR2 SDRAM. The key components needed for podcasting were audio inputs and 512 Mb of memory. A decent microphone was recommended to capture the audio. The Library decided to purchase the Plantronics DSP 500 Microphone Headset, a modestly priced gaming headset with an attached microphone. This allowed users to listen to the audio output without disturbing the entire staff and have only one peripheral instead of two.

In addition to the hardware, the Library purchased a professional licence for QuickTime Pro (for audio capture) and PodcastMaker. PodcastMaker was an inexpensive way to create the chaptering, add images and metadata, upload completed podcasts to the server and create the XML needed for the iTunes podcast subscription feed. PodcastMaker also made it extremely easy to manage multiple podcast series if we decided to branch out. The total cost of the setup was around $2000.

Creating the podcasts

The first step in creating a podcast is to write a script. The librarians were asked to create draft scripts based on either their interest in a specific topic or their knowledge and expertise in a specific area of business resources. These were edited to follow the Kresge Library Dash Podcast format of introduction, overview, content, recap and conclusion. All scripts were written to be read verbatim, leaving little need for improvisation. This created consistency in the style of the writing and facilitated the recording of the podcast. With a good script, it was possible for one librarian to record another librarian's podcast, creating the potential for the Library to produce podcasts more frequently.

The next step is to record the audio portion of the podcast. Once the audio is finished, screen-shots, informational text or other enhancements are added to the podcast, along with any links to resources or further information for a particular image. Theme music is then added to the beginning and end, along with the Kresge Dash logo. Once finished, the podcast files are sent to Computing Services to be uploaded to the Kresge Library section of Ross iTunes U (http://itunes.bus.umich.edu). The new episodes usually appear on the Library iTunes U site within 24 hours. Links to the new episodes are added to the Kresge Library Dash web page where the user can link directly to iTunes, or download the file to view on their computer with QuickTime. The final podcasts run anywhere from 4 to 23 minutes.

From QuickTime to GarageBand

The first podcast was recorded using QuickTime Pro. It was quickly discovered that this program had some limitations. As there was no way to stop and start the recording process and have a single file, it was necessary to record the entire podcast in one take, which proved difficult without a strong script. Once the audio was recorded, the file was opened in PodcastMaker and chapters, images and metadata were added to it. The file was saved in the enhanced podcast file format of m4a. The whole process of recording the first podcast took two days.

After the first podcast was recorded, Apple introduced an updated version of GarageBand that came with a podcast track designed specifically for adding images, links and chapters to the podcast. This made the process of creating the enhanced podcast much quicker as there was now one program that could be used for the entire creation process. The audio was recorded on the voice track, intro and exit music were added on the jingle track, chapters were inserted, titles and hyperlinks added and images dragged onto the podcast track to complete the episode. The podcast was then exported in the correct format (m4a) and saved to the hard drive. The time needed to record and finalize a typical podcast was reduced to about 3-4 hours depending on the length of the script, the number of screen-shots or other images to be created, and the amount of editing to be done to the recorded audio. Completed podcasts range in size from around 3Mb for four and half minutes of enhanced audio podcast up to 235 Mb for 23 minutes of video.

Video + podcasting = vodcasting

After we had created several enhanced podcasts, the Library decided to create a video-based podcast to gauge the effectiveness of video for instruction delivery. With the help of the talented staff from Video Streaming Media Services in Computing Services, an instruction session was recorded without a live audience to allow for mistakes and a more relaxed atmosphere. The session was recorded to digital video tape with a professional-grade video camera. A wireless microphone was used to capture the sound to the video. Once the taping was complete, the tape was given to the Library to complete the editing. The recording was captured to Windows-based digital video editing workstations available in the student computing labs. Adobe Premier was used to edit the video and add enhancements, such as screen-shots and titles.

Editing the video proved to be the most challenging part of creating the podcast. The majority of the problems centred around file format incompatibility. Several different types of image and video files were added to the original footage to enhance the recording, specifically, captured video of the searches being performed by the instructor. Based on time stamps from the original video, the searches were re-created and captured with Camtasia. The resulting video files were individually exported and then imported into the original video in Adobe Premier. This job was complicated by the fact that video editing workstations were not connected to the network or internet and did not have the correct codec for reading the Camtasia files. Also, the Camtasia videos were not of the same quality as the original video.

Once the video was edited, it was exported from Premier as an MPEG 1, the only format which could successfully be read by both QuickTime and iMovie on the Mac, and then imported into iMovie on the Mac. Chapters and links were added at the appropriate points and the final 'vodcast' was exported as a QuickTime movie for use with iTunes or as a stand-alone download.

Student feedback – podcasting survey

After the podcasts and vodcast were created, the Library decided to create a short informal survey to get some feedback on this new instruction format. We especially wanted to know if users liked the format, whether they liked the video or audio podcasts better, and what instructional content they preferred. This informal survey aimed to capture feedback from ten UM Business School students (undergraduates in Business Administration and MBA students). As an incentive, a $10 bookstore gift card was offered to each student upon completion of the survey. The students were asked to listen to ten minutes of any audio podcast (out of seven or so available) and to watch ten minutes of the video podcast (one available). Then they were asked to complete the short questionnaire and to return it to the Library, either in person, or later, when this proved difficult, via e-mail. Interestingly, none of the students chose to listen to the podcasts on an iPod.

Summary of survey results

- The video podcast was preferred by students over classroom instruction and audio podcasts, although the video quality was not as good as they expected.
- Students liked the chaptering feature and the ability to listen to the podcast any time they chose.
- When asked 'What is one thing you remember from the podcast?' several remembered sources or services which called for a librarian's intervention.
- Since they only had to listen to ten minutes of the podcast, the students were asked if they would finish the podcast on their own, or listen to another one. All students said they would finish the current podcast, or another one; or that they had finished the podcast, other podcasts, or the video.
- Students wanted basic library orientation podcasts focused on their particular student status (e.g. MBA, BBA, Evening MBA, etc.).
- Topics suggested for future podcasts leaned toward the practical or in-depth topics – interview preparation, job hunting or digging into one specific database.

What the survey results suggest

Overall, students liked the podcast format as a method for providing library instruction. They felt that podcasting was the most helpful to them for sources that cover practical topics, such as interviewing, or sources that require in-depth instruction. They liked the fact that they could skip around in the instruction and listen or re-listen to parts that were important to them. The results suggest that podcasting is a viable option for providing library instruction and that this service will be used and seen as valuable by the students.

In addition to user feedback, the iTunes statistics show that the podcasts are being used. The eight existing episodes have been downloaded from iTunes a combined total of 442 times through the middle of June 2007. This number does not include downloads from the Library's web page.

Future podcasts

The Kresge Library will move the project out of the pilot phase beginning in the Fall 2007 semester and fully incorporate podcasting into the existing library instruction programme. All new instruction sessions will have a podcast companion episode created. The Library is also exploring the possibility of creating a shorter series of podcast episodes, under four minutes in duration, that will give students a quick overview of a topic or a certain feature of a database or resource. These shorter episodes will require less time commitment from the students and be faster to produce. The Library will continue to create longer, in-depth instruction podcasts on a variety of topics.

Although video was a preferred format for the students, it was extremely time-consuming to create, and new video podcast episodes will be limited. Any new video podcasts to be created will be done directly on the Mac using iMovie or GarageBand to avoid the issues encountered with video during the pilot phase.

For this service to be successful in the future, the Library needs to put more effort into marketing it to our users. None of the students who participated in the survey knew the podcasts existed prior to being contacted about participating in the survey. Future marketing efforts will focus on better placement of podcasts on the Library's website and mentioning the episodes at every classroom instruction session. We will continue to ask our users for feedback about the podcast medium and future topics that they would like to see covered to ensure that the service continues to meet our users' needs.

Conclusion

While the podcasts do enhance the Library's instruction/information literacy programme, the medium presents a few shortcomings, most notably the lack of interaction with a librarian. Students are not able to ask questions or get clarification while listening to the podcast episodes. Each episode discusses how to get additional help from a librarian at the end of the podcast, but none of the methods gives the student the real-time interaction with the librarian that they would receive in a classroom setting. In addition, the medium does require that they have certain software on their workstations, either iTunes or QuickTime.

Overall, the Library sees the podcast series as an excellent way to greatly enhance the topic depth, range, and immediacy of our instructional offerings.

Helpful resources

Podcast Creation Guide,
>   http://images.apple.com/education/solutions/podcasting/pdf/
>   PodcastCreationGuide.pdf.
>   This helpful guide is a bit dated (2005), but still provides good basic information on what a podcast is and the mechanics behind creating one. It also includes helpful information on setting up iTunes for compressing the podcast in the correct file format and basic information on recording in GarageBand.

Podcasting Legal Guide: Rules for the Revolution,
>   http://mirrors.creativecommons.org/Podcasting_Legal_Guide.pdf.
>   A nice guide that covers the legal issues surrounding copyright for content, music, images and distribution of podcasts.

GarageBand 3, www.apple.com/ilife/garageband.
>   Software from Apple for quickly creating enhanced podcasts. It is a part of the iLife '06 suite of software, which includes iMovie.

ProfCast, www.profcast.com.
>   Designed to allow recording and synchronization of lectures with PowerPoint slides for quick conversion into podcasts. For Mac only.

Camtasia, www.techsmith.com/camtasia.asp.
>   Easy to use program for recording on-screen actions and movement. The new version incorporates features that make it easy to publish movies in a format that is compatible with iPods and other portable media players.

PodcastMaker from Lemonz Dream, www.lemonzdream.com/podcastmaker.
A great little utility for adding the metadata, chaptering, URLs and images
to your podcasts. Also helps you manage podcast series and upload directly
to your web space. A free 30-day trial is available. For Mac only.

Chapter 10

PennTags at the University of Pennsylvania

LAURIE ALLEN and MARCELLA BARNHART

PennTags is a social bookmarking tool for locating, organizing and sharing online resources developed by librarians at the University of Pennsylvania (Penn). In addition to serving as a useful research tool, PennTags helps the libraries fulfil Penn President Amy Guttman's vision of the Penn Compact, which challenges the Penn Community to increase access, integrate knowledge and engage locally and globally.

What is PennTags?

PennTags is a user-centric and user-friendly way to organize the academic research process. It acknowledges that most resources are either fully digital or have digital representations such as catalogue records or database citations. Because it fits easily into the landscape of digital resources, PennTags provides many of the benefits of any other kind of social bookmarking system, such as del.icio.us or ma.gnolia.com. Using a web-based system frees the user to work from any machine and offers more flexibility in organizing resources. By using tags instead of folders, users can assign multiple identities to a single resource, creating access points for subjects, geographic coverage, authors, formats and the like – whatever makes sense for their research needs.

Rather than simply drawing data from library systems and the public web into the PennTags environment, PennTags also pulls user-created content into the public view of the library catalogue. The PennTags content is retrieved dynamically when a user chooses to view a full or brief record in the catalogue. It includes whatever content the user included in the original posting, such as tags and annotations. Not only does this have the potential to add richness to the information available on the catalogue record, but it also allows related resources from within PennTags to be serendipitously discovered by catalogue users who may not have been aware of PennTags otherwise. However, PennTags has advantages over commercial systems in that it is designed to be used with library resources, including Penn's online catalogues, databases and Open-URL resolver (SFX). While systems like CiteULike and Connotea do focus on the academic or scholarly research communities, PennTags is publisher agnostic and designed to be used by anyone in the Penn community, regardless of their area of interest.

PennTags history

PennTags was initially developed in August 2005 in response to a request from a Cinema Studies faculty member for a wiki to use as part of one of his classes. Each student in his class was required to submit an annotated bibliography about a film, and the professor wanted a way for students to easily share their work with their classmates and with future film students. After discussion with public services librarians and the library's Director of Information Technology and Digital Development (ITADD), they decided to do something a little more ambitious. Rather than creating a wiki that would be limited to a particular class, the library would create a system that allowed the bibliographies to be more broadly shared, and that would have the potential to be used for applications other than this class assignment. The preliminary code for the application was written in a few days by the director of the ITADD group and the tool was immediately launched in beta form for testing and use by the students enrolled in the target classes. Since the initial proof of concept, the underlying structure of the application has changed somewhat in response to user feedback, and to add greater functionality. A team of librarians, comprised mainly of public services librarians, but also including a member from cataloguing, was brought in to work with ITADD's digital projects librarian and web designer to develop the system for broader institutional use.

Although it is not part of the MARC record or the official catalogue entry, presenting user-created content in the catalogue has been viewed as controversial by some members of the library community. The PennTags team has received many e-mail messages from other librarians asking about the motivations behind developing PennTags. Many of them seem to assume that PennTags is a grand experiment in user behaviour or a bold statement about the relevance of traditional cataloguing and classification. While there is certainly a great deal of potential for interesting research to be done in how people use PennTags, and in how folksonomies may differ from traditional classification, in reality PennTags is simply intended to be a tool to help students, faculty and staff manage and share their research. So, while PennTags was not designed with its uses as an information literacy tool in mind, a look at its current and potential benefits shows that user-created tags and content in the library system can help students become more information literate.

Benefits of PennTags for information literacy

Though PennTags has not yet been marketed or offered to any major audiences at Penn beyond the media studies courses, it has found devoted users in the life sciences, humanities, and social sciences. It has also provided a tool for Penn librarians to create on-the-fly research guides when they are consulting with students. Through its RSS capabilities, librarians can also create more traditional research guides that are easily updated. To aid in the use of PennTags for academic research, Penn librarians have developed a one-session class that includes information on PennTags as part of a comprehensive set of tools to make research more efficient. Since PennTags is a generic research tool designed to be used for any project, overviews of PennTags have been included in many other library instruction sessions as well.

At its simplest, information literacy is the ability to locate, evaluate and use information resources. Through the process of assigning tags to PennTags' posts, students need to think about how the resources they have identified fit into their broader academic mission, and are similar to, or different from, other resources. By exploring what others have posted and tagged, students can begin to gain an understanding of the vocabulary and structure of a particular field of enquiry, and can see how their own interests fit into that field. Because PennTags has been used heavily in particular classes in film and media studies, the PennTags system is particularly rich in resources related to film, copyright and media studies.

Looking at posts that are already there before they begin their projects can give students a sense of the jargon in their field of enquiry, and of the types of sources that are appropriate for the assignment. In addition, assigning tags to resources forces students to think purposefully about how a resource might be useful to them, helping them refine and consider their questions.

PennTags directly relates to Standard Two, Performance Indicator Five of ACRL's Information Literacy Standards for Higher Education (Association of College and Research Libraries, 2000) which states that 'The information literate student extracts, records and manages the information and its sources'. PennTags gives students a robust tool for keeping track of their research process. The PennTags bookmarklet simplifies the process so that students, without needing to be bothered with the mechanics of extracting information, can readily return to a resource, i.e. no more copying and pasting or e-mailing URLs to resources. Students can easily cast a very wide net when they begin their research by capturing many potential resources in PennTags; these can be culled or further developed as their research progresses. The annotation feature gives students the opportunity to record notes about the resource and how it relates to their projects. These notes could range from general information about the type of journals or data that can be found in a particular database to a detailed analysis of the author's arguments from a specific journal article. Posts and annotations can be easily edited, allowing students to change or add to a post as they get further into their research process. By having students use PennTags to record and document the resources used in their research process, faculty can confirm that students have met Standard Five, Performance Indicator Two of the ACRL Standards (2000): 'The information literate student follows laws, regulations, institutional policies, and etiquette related to the access and use of information resources.'

User reactions and feedback

PennTags has not been aggressively marketed to the Penn community. As mentioned above, it has been used by faculty as part of assignments in particular classes, but has not been offered to the entire Penn community. As a result, the uptake of the system has been relatively small. There are approximately 880 people who have posted at least one item to PennTags out of a potential community of 50,000.

PennTags 2.0

A new version of PennTags is currently in development. This new version will include features that encourage collaboration among PennTags users, and that make it easier for users to change and update their tags and posts. The new version will be marketed to the Penn community, and we expect to learn a great deal from the uses of PennTags in that time.

Reference

Association of College and Research Libraries (2000) *Information Literacy Competency Standards for Higher Education*, American Library Association, www.ala.org/ala/acrl/acrlstandards/informationliteracycompetency.htm.

Chapter 11

Sparking Flickrs of insight into controlled vocabularies and subject searching

CAMERON HOFFMAN and
SARAH POLKINGHORNE

> I shall also call the whole, consisting of language and the actions
> into which it is woven, the 'language-game'.
>
> (Wittgenstein, 1967, 5e).

Introduction

Flickr, created by Ludicorp and currently owned by Yahoo!, is one of the most popular photo-sharing applications on the world wide web. Flickr (www.flickr.com), enables users to upload their photos into online galleries. Flickr users describe their photos through image tagging, a natural-language process in which users can ascribe any combination of words or phrases to photos in order to make them retrievable. This chapter describes an information literacy instructional activity in which the tagging capacity of Flickr helps students learn the distinctions between natural and controlled vocabularies as well as the potential advantages of subject searching. We have used the Flickr activity to enhance information literacy classes, in the hope of moving beyond merely technical database training sessions to deeper learning experiences that allow for a rich discussion of metadata, vocabularies and searching by subject heading. By participating in the Flickr activity, students discover that 'Googling', or searching strictly by keyword, is not always an ideal research strategy. Because of the Flickr activity, students have been able to get a sense of the richness and precision possible through searching by subject heading or the controlled vocabularies of database thesauri. We begin our case study by briefly situating the tagging activity within the context of library patrons' historical tendencies to search by keyword rather than by subject heading or other controlled vocabularies.

Instructional context: the difficulties of teaching and learning how to search by subject

Subject searching – that is, navigating the library catalogue's controlled subject headings or a database's thesaurus terms, rather than searching solely by keyword – is difficult to master as a concept, let alone as a skill. Our central proposal here is that today's popular social web tools, particularly photo-sharing applications, can serve librarians very well in their efforts to teach controlled vocabularies and subject headings in an effective and engaging way. To begin, however, this chapter introduces some of what librarians know about users' experiences of subject searching.

There is a body of research that endeavours to measure and interpret patrons' long-standing struggles with subject searching. Such research began soon after online catalogues were introduced in the 1980s. Researchers also began to examine patrons' keyword searching practices. They discovered that while subject searching was in decline, keyword searching was on the increase (Larson, 1991).

It may seem surprising that these findings predate the web, which enables and encourages keyword searching like no search tool before it. Sure enough, today's researchers are discovering the effects of web searching habits on users' attempts to find what they need in the library catalogue and databases. Analysis of catalogue transaction logs, for example, has revealed that increasing numbers of patrons search the catalogue in ways that would be more successful in other contexts, such as web searching (Yu and Young, 2004).

Meanwhile, many users express confusion and anxiety over subject searching. When asked to perform subject searches of a library catalogue, they are more likely to experience problems finding information than those who use other catalogue search methods, and they are also more likely to express a low opinion of the catalogue's organization (Halcoussis et al., 2002). Subject searching has always been frustrating for many users. It seems that the web has exacerbated and complicated these frustrations.

None of this will come as any great surprise to librarians who have observed their patrons struggling to find information in catalogues and databases. But what hope does this leave for the effective teaching of controlled vocabularies and subject searching? On this front, the web may seem to have made matters worse for both librarians and users. But it also provides us with a new set of tools that millions of users enjoy every day, and which, thanks to tagging, can be used to introduce the concept of controlled vocabularies and the practice of subject searching. These tools include Facebook, YouTube, del.icio.us and, in this case, Flickr.

Flickr as teaching tool
Technical considerations

We would like to make a number of preliminary technical points regarding how we regularly prepare and implement the Flickr activity. First, the photographs we use in the activity are mainly those we ourselves have taken, so as to avoid any copyright concerns. We have typically photographed various campus landmarks and everyday scenes and objects. Second, we have always taught this activity in a computer lab, where students have individual access to the web - and to Flickr - from their own computers. The activity could be adapted to a space other than a computer lab by using other resources, such as PowerPoint, handouts or slips of paper, or even by using a whiteboard or chalkboard. Third, we have implemented the Flickr activity mainly with undergraduate and graduate students in university information literacy sessions, though we believe that the activity could easily be adapted to other library user communities as well.

Activity description

1   Before the class, the information literacy instructor creates an account at the Flickr website and uploads a number of digital photos into it. (The exact number is up to the instructor: we have used as few as eight and as many as 25.) No tags are ascribed to the photos prior to the class, although the instructor may give each image a title and a description.
2   The instructor presents the Flickr account, with its gallery, to students. The class receives temporary access - the password - to the Flickr account. (We change this password immediately after each class so as to prevent vandalism of the account.)

3   The instructor informs the students how to navigate the Flickr interface to tag photos.

4   The instructor asks the students, working individually, to enter the Flickr account and tag the photos in the gallery. The instruction given to the students is that they must try to tag the images *so that they can be retrieved by other Flickr users.*

5   The instructor asks the students to begin tagging. During this time, the instructor can tell students that if they hit the Refresh or Reload buttons on their web browsers, they can see in real time the tags their colleagues are making. The students tag the images for several minutes, after which the instructor calls a halt to the activity. At this point, each of the gallery's images now bears tags, but there is no way for anyone in the classroom to determine which students have entered specific tags.

6   The class then inspects each photo. As a class, the students discuss and assess the tags. The instructor can facilitate discussion around a variety of questions:
   • Are the tags *accurate*? (Do they make sense? Do they actually describe the object?)
   • Are the tags *meaningful*? (Is the tag understood by everyone, or only by the person who tagged it?)
   • Are the tags *correctly made*? (Are they properly spelled? Are there observable variations in the spellings?)
   • Do the tags make the photos *more retrievable*?

7   The instructor then introduces the idea that subject headings in library catalogues and the indexing terms in database thesauri are, to an extent, much like tags of Flickr photos. A cataloguer 'tags' books and audiovisual items, and an indexer 'tags' articles in a database. The difference, though, between the tagging in Flickr and professional cataloguing and indexing lies in the nature of the language: in Flickr, the language is *natural*, originating in the users' vernacular, while in library catalogues and most databases the language is *controlled*, as specifically co-ordinated words or phrases are used to describe the 'aboutness' of the object.

8   The activity can proceed in various directions at this point, depending on the teaching outcomes of the instructor. One possibility is that students could receive more technical instruction on the arrangement of subject headings or indexing terms. Another possibility is that the

class could move into a discussion of the accuracy and usefulness of various catalogue headings. The class could even try changing their Flickr tags using the controlled vocabulary of Library of Congress subject headings.

Tagging matters: student discoveries from the activity

Students involved in the Flickr tagging activity have made discoveries and observations about tagging, cataloguing and indexing, and gained awareness of some of the issues involved in accurately and meaningfully describing information-bearing objects. Some of the most compelling student discoveries are noted here.

The importance of correct spelling

Right away, students have critiqued colleagues' tags that have been misspelled. For example, students noted that the tag 'hibiskis' could never make a photo of a Hawaiian hibiscus plant retrievable. Students discussed how word processor spell-check programs and Google's search suggestion feature – 'Did you mean: *hibiscus*' – have made them less careful about checking their own spelling. Some students noted that when it comes to spelling, library catalogues and most databases are not as forgiving as Microsoft Word and Google. These insights can enable the instructor to reinforce the importance of correct spelling when searching catalogues and databases.

Limitations and benefits of 'insider language'

We have occasionally included photos of family pets in the activity's Flickr gallery. Students have sometimes used their imaginations to ascribe names to the animals in these photos. For example, an image of an Irish Setter dog has been variously tagged 'Rover', 'Spot' and 'Big Red', even though the students do not know the true name of the animal in the photo. In post-activity discussion, students realized that even if they did tag the photo with the dog's real name, this would not significantly enhance the photo's findability, since most Flickr users would search for the image using only search terms such as 'dog', 'Irish Setter' or 'hunting dog'. As students assess their tags' 'insider language' – words that only they or their friends find meaningful – they begin to realize the complexities with which cataloguers and indexers wrestle in pursuit of globally meaningful subject terms. Consequently, students have come to appreciate the controlled vocabularies of subject headings and thesauri terms, and endeavour to use them in their research. Other students have argued for the possible advantages of folksonomic tagging, through which users can create and share meaning through search terms only comprehensible among their contemporaries.

Privileging the concrete over the metaphorical

One of the Flickr images we used is of a standard institutional wall clock that reads '7:38'. Students have typically tagged this image 'clock' or '7:38', but some students have tagged it 'time'. Discussions about this image have involved students thinking about the predominance of more concrete terms in cataloguing and indexing. One student spoke about how her search for biographies of Saddam Hussein had failed because she had used the term 'dictator', rather than a more concrete – and less value-laden – subject heading such as 'Presidents – Iraq – Biography'.

Cultural biases in language

Occasionally, the Flickr activity has led to student critique of the cultural biases of some subject headings. In one class, students tagged an image of the fictitious pig Wilbur, a character from the children's book *Charlotte's Web*, with the terms 'pig', 'Wilbur', 'Charlotte's Web' and even 'E. B. White', the book's author. Students generally agreed that these were good tags, because they made the pig image highly retrievable. However, one student from a particular religious background indicated that he would choose the tag 'unclean'. This led to a discussion of how individuals from different cultures can have significantly differing perspectives on information-bearing objects and the immense challenge of cataloguing and indexing in a way that is both acceptable and accessible for most searchers. In another class, the discussion revolved around the controversial Library of Congress subject heading 'Indians of North America', which strikes most students in our classes (we work mainly with Canadian university students) as obsolete, exclusionary and even racist.

Conclusion

The Flickr activity is fun. Students enjoy tagging and then critiquing their peers' tags. There is no way to know which students are responsible for which tags, and students find this anonymity encouraging: even when tags are criticized, no one is singled out. Amidst all of the fun, however, the Flickr activity also facilitates student learning on several levels. The activity helps students gain sensitivity about how information-bearing objects are described. It gives students a sense of the differences between their own natural vocabularies and the controlled vocabularies of catalogues and databases. It introduces students to the challenges of answering the question 'what is this *about?*' In our classes, the Flickr activity has served as a reliably effective and engaging tool to introduce both the concept of controlled vocabularies and the skill of subject searching.

Acknowledgements

We would like to express our gratitude to Rumi Graham (University of Lethbridge Library), Deborah Hicks (University of Alberta Libraries) and Dr Heidi Julien (University of Alberta, School of Library and Information Studies) for their assistance during the writing of this chapter.

References

Halcoussis, D., Halverson, A. L., Lowenberg, A. D. and Lowenberg, S. (2002) An Empirical Analysis of Web Catalog User Experiences, *Information Technology and Libraries,* **21** (4), 148–57.

Larson, R. R. (1991) The Decline of Subject Searching: long-term trends and patterns of index use in an online catalogue, *Journal of the American Society for Information Science,* **42** (3), 197–215.

Wittgenstein, L. (1967) *Philosophical Investigations,* Basil Blackwell, trans. G. E. M. Anscombe.

Yu, H. and Young, M. (2004) The Impact of Web Search Engines on Subject Searching in OPAC, *Information Technology and Libraries,* **23** (4), 168–80.

Chapter 12

Joining the YouTube conversation to teach information literacy

SUSAN ARIEW

In the summer of 2006 the University of South Florida's Tampa Library embarked on a new project to create a pilot video for instructional purposes, using the talents of a YouTube amateur video blogger. The production of the pilot video, and another following it, eventually created momentum for the library in embracing YouTube for hosting instructional videos. How and why such a project could become an agent for change will be the subject of this chapter.

Getting started

Librarians at the University of South Florida (USF), an institution serving about 45,000 students, with 35,000 on campus, teach information literacy in a variety of settings: some of them have had experience teaching LIS 2005, a three-credit information literacy class for undergraduates, in the library school; the majority teach single instruction sessions and orientations for students at all levels; but the bulk involve classes for first-year students. The motivation behind creating a pilot video did not originate from some grand plan to reach 'millennials' on YouTube with an information literacy message; it started simply from the desire to see more readily available short videos on the internet that could be used in the library instruction classroom. There were precious few interesting, entertaining, or engaging short videos relating to information literacy. The best video available on the topic of information literacy was a short, 15-minute streaming video entitled

'E-Literate' (New Literacies, 2000). 'E-Literate' was used in many classrooms in the USA at the time it came out in 2000. It highlighted the dangers of not properly evaluating one's sources, especially internet resources, in finding information. 'E-Literate' also offered some astonishing statistics about information overload and the information explosion created by the internet. However, 'E-Literate', as good as it was as a teaching tool, had become dated by 2006. It had been made before Web 2.0 technologies; the statistics it gave were pre-blogs, pre-social networking websites, and pre-YouTube, all of which have revolutionized internet use and interactions among users.

Using Web 2.0 technologies

As YouTube, Google videos, and other video-hosting websites became more popular, librarians at USF looking for good multimedia products to enhance library instruction discovered that materials posted on the web were more current and entertaining than the 'E-Literate' video. YouTube videos were particularly useful because their brevity made them ideal for 50–90 minute class sessions. For example, Steven Colbert's clip 'Wikiality' (2006) provided a terrific satirical lesson about the limitations of the Wikipedia and the need to think critically about using it as a source of information. Another clip, 'EPIC 2014' (Sloan and Thompson, 2005), offers a futuristic look at the changes in the news business such as the collapse of the fourth estate and reliable news reporting. A more recent clip that has been circulating on the Web is 'glumbert', which offers startling statistics about the future of the workforce (Fisch, 2006). The Library of Congress Penn and Teller video on YouTube illustrates primary sources in a very engaging and humorous way when they take a look at the Houdini collection (mfilms, 2006).

Thus, the first step in terms of joining the Web 2.0 conversation was for librarians to become active consumers of innovations or new technologies and to find ways to apply them to teaching information literacy in library instruction classes. Web 2.0 applications taught users that interaction on the web did not just have to be one way – that much of what is published can become a conversation, not just a statement. YouTube, and other video-hosting websites, also proposed to users that anyone can create and post videos and therefore, if users do not find what they want on the internet they can create it themselves.

Creating videos for library instruction

In the process of using YouTube videos for classroom purposes, the next step for librarians becoming literate with this new medium was to become publishers or contributors. Creating videos for the library instruction classroom began at USF as a summer project involving a student volunteer, who happened to enjoy making YouTube videos, and a group of interested librarians. Two librarians and the student volunteer spent time brainstorming and listing instructional objectives for the project. What did they want students to learn in a short video? What scenarios or stories might illustrate the teaching ideas in the video?

Once there was a concept for the video, the next step was to write a script for it and find the right people to be part of the video cast. At that point USF's Associate Director of Reference and Library Instruction organized a team of librarians to work on the project. It consisted of two librarians, a graduate student in library science and two student volunteers. The script was a collaborative effort of the team and thus embraced both the undergraduate student perspective and the teaching objectives of the professional librarians.

Challenges

Because this was a new project, the team had difficulty in obtaining proper equipment for the project. They ended up borrowing a video camera that was not state of the art from a central campus facility. The audio was not consistently adequate. There were other problems with casting and shooting the video in the library when others would not be disturbed. The group had to rely on the student volunteer's computer and editing equipment, since he was not part of the library staff and could not use the equipment in the library. Despite all the challenges and frustrations in creating the first video, 'Databases' was moderately successful. One of more engaging features of 'Databases' was the music used in it. However, that became an issue for the library too because it was copyrighted material. The library could not host or actively promote a video on its own website if it violated copyright. Ultimately, the student video blogger posted 'Databases' to YouTube on his own account (Ariew, 2006a).

Classroom applications

'Databases' was used in the fall of 2006 individually in library instruction classes at USF as an 'icebreaker' for basic classes to engage students in discussions about information literacy. Student and faculty reactions to the 'Databases' video were mixed. As with most teaching tools, the video was successful in the classroom when it was properly introduced and integrated into the learning objectives of the lessons. Once it became part of a well designed classroom activity, it seemed effective. Because it was on YouTube, a link could be provided to it from courseware so that faculty members could use it in orienting students to the world of library resources and tools.

Members of the video team, having enjoyed moderate success in the creation of 'Databases', went on to create another pilot video, 'The Chronicles of Libraria', just for fun (Ariew and Bishop, 2006). This video (see Figure 12.1), the creative idea of one member of the USF library faculty, was a spoof based on the *Saturday Night Live* rap video, 'Lazy Sunday' (Lazy Sunday, 2007). 'Lazy Sunday' featured two college boys rapping about cupcakes and *The Chronicles of Narnia*; USF's video featured two college boys rapping about smoothies and the library. It included an anti-plagiarism theme.

Figure 12.1 A still from 'Chronicles of Libraria'.
Reproduced with thanks by permission of David Ariew.

While 'The Chronicles of Libraria' was a lot less instructional in content, it was featured nationally in *ALA Direct*, an online weekly newsletter from the American Library Association and thus received a lot of attention from librarians across the country. Unlike 'Databases' this video was better quality and easier to produce because the library staff supported it more actively with access to state-of-the-art video camera equipment. Moreover, 'Chronicles' was linked directly on the USF Library home page because it was copyright compliant.

The impact of 'Databases' and 'The Chronicles of Libraria'

As stated earlier, copyright issues for the library caused the first pilot video to be posted only to YouTube. USF also hosted 'The Chronicles of Libraria' on YouTube because of very limited server space. Putting videos on YouTube meant that USF Tampa Library didn't have to purchase additional server space and host these large files even if they could create them. The unintended consequences of hosting the videos on YouTube was the interest that they created from the library community at large. For example, a librarian from the Hillsborough Community College Library at Ybor City asked if she could have permission to use and modify the source video for 'Databases' so she could shorten it but include the parts she thought were best instructionally for her classes.

Several libraries linked directly to both pilot videos on YouTube and have featured them on their websites. In the spring of 2007, both videos were featured in a presentation at LOEX, 'Keeping Up With the YouTube Generation' (Ariew, 2006) and another video was created and posted on YouTube, 'YouTube, Librarians, and Me' (Ariew, 2006b), this time for the conference presentation. In this YouTube video, the student blogger talks about his fascination with YouTube, how he started creating amateur videos, and his involvement with the USF Tampa Library. He also details the kind of equipment he used to create videos and to edit them for a librarian audience. The response by librarians to the presentation at LOEX was positive; it continued the conversation about the role of libraries in creating videos. Thus the videos have contributed as object lessons to the library community and have created interesting conversations about what libraries can do to bring information literacy concepts to students through new digital tools and Web 2.0 technologies.

Moving forward: where USF Tampa Library is now

A year later, in the summer of 2007, the USF Tampa Library hired the YouTube video blogger for the summer to be a podcast/vodcast editor to help them populate the new iTunes University space as part of a new Web 2.0 venture the university has undertaken with Apple. The library began the summer with only three podcasts posted on the library's iTunes space. By the fall of 2007, the library had created and posted over 100 podcasts and videocasts, mostly with the help of the student assistant. Among the new videos created for instruction was an entertaining and humorous tour of the USF Tampa Library (Ariew, Torrance and D'Avanza, 2007) and an instructional five-minute hybrid workshop video (Ariew and Ariew, 2007) about subject guides. Also created were videos or unique podcasts of library collections, oral histories and cultural events, all sponsored by the USF Tampa Library. While the pilot videos were not blockbuster successes as information literacy tools, their creation served to move the USF Tampa library forward in many ways, such as:

- the hiring of an expert audio/video editor/producer
- more support for creating new videos
- buy-in from all parts of the library in creating and supporting new podcast/vodcast productions
- the library setting up its own YouTube account to post videos
- plans for hiring a full-time instructional technology expert
- obtaining more dedicated local server space for hosting multimedia instructional products that can link to faculty course management software.

To find local talented video bloggers, in the fall of 2007, the USF Tampa library sponsored a Video Contest, knowing that talented amateurs might be able to create additional videos for library instruction. The contest is not just a talent search. It is also an opportunity to educate the students about copyright issues and the need for including the library and information literacy as subject matter for video bloggers.

Lessons learned

The USF librarians learned from the YouTube experience that, in keeping up with Web 2.0 technologies, librarians needed to become Web 2.0 consumers and then collaborate with others who are very much a part of the world of YouTube. Working with a student volunteer who possessed new skill sets and literacies, the librarians learned that they did not need to know how to do everything themselves. However, they did need to learn what skills they were looking for in creating a place for new employees who can move the library forward, and that required active involvement with the medium. What began as a project to reach and teach young people about information literacy has become something that taught librarians about the literacies of Web 2.0, its accompanying technology and the human capital to make things happen. Moreover, it has, in fact, created a conversation on many levels about the library, technology and information literacy. Finally, USF Tampa librarians learned from the YouTube experience that posting their videos touched many librarians who were also looking for ways to apply this new medium to their work. This led to librarians joining the conversation professionally and sharing their work on a larger scale than just locally. And this is what the Web 2.0 experience is all about.

References

Ariew, D. (2006a) 'Databases!', YouTube,
    www.youtube.com/watch?v=nik3pyJwaYI.
Ariew, D. (2006b) 'YouTube, Librarians, and Me', YouTube,
    www.youtube.com/watch?v=F9Sw7qnYZXo.
Ariew D. and Ariew, S. (2007) 'Subject Guides',
    www.lib.usf.edu/learn/tutorials/subjectguides.mov.
Ariew, D. and Bishop, W. (2006) 'The Chronicles of Libraria', YouTube,
    www.youtube.com/watch?v=mZR6WkbPK8M.
Ariew, D, Torrence, M. and D'Avanza, M. (2007) 'Tampa Library Tour 2007',
    www.lib.usf.edu/learn/tours/tampalibrarytour2007.mov.
Ariew, S. (2006) 'Keeping up With the YouTube Generation', LOEX 2007, San
    Diego, California, May 4, 2006, www.csusm.edu/acarr/materials.
Colbert, S. (2006) 'Wikiality', www.comedycentral.com.
Fisch, K. (2007) 'glumbert' (Shift Happens), http://glumbert.com/media/shift.
'Lazy Sunday' (2007) Wikipedia, http://en.wikipedia.org/wiki/Lazy_Sunday.

mlfilms (2006) 'Memory and Imagination: new pathways to the Library of
    Congress', YouTube, www.youtube.com/watch?v=R_PkSfIjlTE.
New Literacies Video (2000) 'E-Literate',
    www.newliteracies.gseis.ucla.edu/video/index.html.
Sloan, R. and Thompson, R. (2005) 'Epic 2014',
    http://epic.makingithappen.co.uk.

Chapter 13

Going Beyond Google at The Open University

JO PARKER

The explosion in Web 2.0 tools, the number of blogs, and the increase in MySpace pages are stark indicators that the environment in which information professionals are operating looks very different from the way it looked as recently as two years ago. At the Open University (OU) Library we have responded to these changes by producing a new course, TU120 Beyond Google, in collaboration with academic colleagues from the Faculty of Technology.

Background

Between 2002 and 2005 the OU offered a course called U120 MOSAIC (Making Sense of Information in the Connected Age). Beyond Google started life as a suggestion for an updated version of U120. However, it quickly became clear that what we had intended as a relatively straightforward 'refreshing' of the U120 content wasn't appropriate given the marked changes in the information landscape. Beyond Google includes more typically 'academic' content, rather than revolving around skills development, which had been our focus with U120. It was inevitable, then, that the course should feature some of the Web 2.0 tools that are becoming part and parcel of our interactions with information. We have, however, tried to take a holistic view, where the tools are inseparable from the skills, and have been able to introduce students to a range of Web 2.0 technologies as a result.

Beyond Google sits within the OU's Relevant Knowledge programme, which includes other short courses on such diverse topics as digital photography and computer security. The course is worth ten points at level one (entry level). Given the subject matter, it is also entirely online, with support provided by a team of moderators via a system of online forums. The course runs over ten weeks twice a year, in October and May. One considerable benefit of working within the OU's course production system is the luxury of teaching time. A short course at the OU lasts 100 hours over ten weeks, as opposed to the 45 minutes many of us are used to when meeting students at induction. This has given us opportunities to explore technologies and develop activities that we had not previously been able to consider, not least of which is persuading students to explore the possibilities of search beyond search engines, hence the course name.

Web 2.0 tools

As we started our rewrite, it became clear that the approach we had taken in U120 was no longer appropriate. U120 taught students about information searching as a step-by-step process, using SCONUL's Seven Pillars model (1999) as a basis. When writing TU120, we had begun to recognize that the environment students operate in is increasingly complex, with a rich array of tools that we could use to enhance our teaching of the search process. That said, the learning outcomes of the course still draw heavily on the model, which underpins rather than drives the content.

The eight teaching weeks of the course comprise:

- World of information (covers the information landscape, search engines, the hidden web, advertising, accountability and retail)
- Becoming a smart searcher (how to make best use of Google features)
- Where Google doesn't go (why search engines can't find everything, and an introduction to tools that can)
- Making sense of information (where information comes from; the information supply chain)
- Evaluating information (how to be a discerning user of information)
- Organizing and sharing your information (how to use social bookmarks, desktop search tools and bibliographic software)
- User-generated content (all about blogs, wikis, YouTube and Flickr)
- Keeping up to date (RSS feeds, e-mail alerts).

As a result of working on TU120 Beyond Google, we have realized that there is a wealth of information literacy teaching that can be conveyed using Web 2.0 technologies, and that these tools and services are a natural extension to the teaching that we have always delivered. Most of the teaching in TU120 is a combination of introducing students to the tools, and then using them to highlight aspects of information literacy. The course is activity driven; students are encouraged to experiment with the tools, and then share their experiences with colleagues in the forums. There are also interactive activities (e.g. ideas bank, voting, quizzes and animations – used sparingly, to take accessibility into account) to convey particular aspects of learning. For example, students read material about the open access movement, and then vote on whether it is a good thing or not; an animation is used to illustrate the thought processes behind planning a search, and quizzes are used at particular points in the course to reinforce the learning.

The phenomenon of user-generated content is a recurring theme throughout the course. For example, blogs and wikis have provided us with a wide range of opportunities to explore many aspects of information literacy. Students cover what blogs are and how to set one up should they choose to, but there are also activities designed to illustrate the importance of evaluation in relation to blogs. Students are also encouraged to use blogs to keep themselves up to date, in terms of having immediate access to the thoughts of experts, and then subscribing to their blogs using RSS feeds. Learning about wikis and Wikipedia allows students to consider issues around provenance and objectivity. For example, one activity focuses on getting students to find an entry in Wikipedia which might be less than objective and share it, and their reasons for mentioning it, with fellow students. Blogs and wikis are also discussed in the context of 'the shape of the literature', as examples of how they are changing the way information is produced as part of the research supply chain.

A section on social bookmarking tools such as BlinkList, Furl and del.icio.us enables us to introduce concepts around storing and organizing information, and tagging. The tools are used as a gentle way in to storing references to start building good practice, which leads in to the use of more complex referencing tools such as RefWorks or Zotero. Introducing students to Flickr allows us to address issues around creating new knowledge, and particularly concerns about privacy and ethics. Discussions in the student forums indicate that this is something students are starting to take seriously, focusing on what level of information they are willing to share, and how they react to the notion of public versus private information. We do not often know the demographic of our students, though a 'typical' Open University student is often older than an undergraduate elsewhere; it would be interesting to discover whether there is any correlation between these privacy concerns and the concepts of digital native/digital immigrant.

Web 2.0 tools tend to lend themselves particularly well to demonstrating how to keep yourself up to date. Students experiment with RSS feeds and aggregators such as Bloglines, Pageflakes and Netvibes, and explore the personalization functionality offered by Google. We also practise what we preach, using RSS to deliver the latest course news.

One of the things we were keen to do in the course was to use audio and podcasts. Each student receives an MP3 player when they register (possibly a bit of an incentive), preloaded with interviews with so-called 'silver surfers', researchers and a group of teenagers, talking about their interactions with information. This helps to give the skills a 'voice' in that hopefully students can relate their own experiences to one or other of the groups. We also offer short clips of downloadable audio, released to students in the study week relevant to the content; the continued and sustained effort involved in producing and maintaining a regular podcast that students can subscribe to, to help keep the course fresh, has so far defeated us, but it is something we are keen to do.

Underpinning all the course content is guidance on how to search for material whatever its format, and subsequently, how to work out what it is you are looking at and evaluate it confidently.

Assessment

The Web 2.0 aspects of the course are particularly prominent in the assessment. There are two parts to the assessment: a multiple choice assignment at the halfway point, covering material studied in the first five weeks of the course, and a longer end-of-course assessment. Here students are asked to illustrate their use of some of the Web 2.0 tools and demonstrate the skills they have learned throughout the course. Students are asked to decide on a search topic of their own choosing, and plan and carry out a search for material using subscription and 'free' web resources. They document their search plans and progress, and comment on their findings.

Students then choose a social bookmarking tool to store and organize the items they have found, and comment on the features they find most useful. They then use the material they have found to produce a short report on their topic, to include citations and a bibliography. They document their evaluation of the material, justifying its inclusion in the report. Finally, they are asked to identify how they are going to keep up to date with their topic, using tools of their choice (e.g. blogs, RSS, e-mail alerting services), giving reasons why the method they have chosen is the most appropriate for their needs.

Students have told us they particularly appreciate being given a free choice of topic, and every assignment is different as a result, with subjects ranging from hobbies to work-related situations. One student commented: 'My enthusiasm for the current Open University course that I'm studying . . . has been revitalized with an excellent ECA question. We're allowed to choose our own search topic. I find it far more rewarding to work on a subject that I can relate to rather than having one set.'

Lessons learned

In terms of lessons learned, writing and offering work up to our academic colleagues for scrutiny was by turns disheartening ('too "librarian!"') and immensely rewarding. One benefit of working with academic colleagues from a different but related discipline is that it is refreshing to bounce ideas around with, and be challenged by, people who have a different take on what Web 2.0 is all about. Academic freedom and the official backing of the university gave us time to experiment, which a commitment to service delivery does not always allow. Finding out about Web 2.0 tools has led us to change our practices and informs work in other areas; TU120 content finds its way into other teaching materials, both online and face to face, while one colleague is now a self-confessed 'social bookmarks junkie'!

Student reaction to the course has been positive on the whole, and many are particularly enthusiastic about the opportunities to experiment with the Web 2.0 tools: 'I have learnt a considerable amount, especially with regard to user-generated content, tagging and keeping up to date, all of which will be of great benefit to me while using the internet.' Some have also commented on the value of the tools both for their personal interests and in the workplace, which is encouraging.

Future plans

We have lots of ideas for what we might do in future, such as a higher level course, for example: what would a more advanced version of information literacy in the Web 2.0 environment look like? The commitment to keeping the course up to date is inevitably an issue when new tools and services are emerging all the time. We manage this in part by providing a forum where the students can put interesting links they have found, and by posting items to the course website news area related to the study weeks. This also provides us with a useful means of refreshing content for the next presentation of the course; however, while this means that the content is never stale and is always up to date, it is sometimes difficult to pinpoint the tools that are going to be the 'next big thing'. However, by producing this course we have acknowledged that these tools (or their successors, at least) are here to stay and being used enthusiastically by all; as librarians we have the analytical and teaching skills to foster best practice. It is inevitable that they should be part of our information landscape.

References

SCONUL (1999) *Information Skills in Higher Education: a SCONUL position paper*, www.sconul.ac.uk/groups/information_literacy/papers/Seven_pillars2.pdf.
TU120 Beyond Google (2007), www.openuniversity.co.uk/tu120 [taster site].

Chapter 14

Using Web 2.0 to enhance the Staffordshire University Assignment Survival Kit (ASK)

JULIE ADAMS, ALISON POPE and
GEOFF WALTON

Introduction

ASK is a web-based tool designed to support undergraduate students encountering their first assignment. In June 2007 it was awarded the CILIP University, College and Research Group (UC&R) Award for Innovation. ASK is the work of the Information Literacy Project Working Group within Staffordshire University (SU) Information Services (IS). The ASK team includes librarians, information professionals, IT developers and e-learning experts. The software was created by the complete adaptation of open source software used by the University of Minnesota in their Assignment Calculator. Scripts were re-used and rewritten to allow local relevance, for example, UK date and time format. The software, viewable at www.staffs.ac.uk/ask, links to a number of useful learning support web pages both internal and external to the University (see Figure 14.1 on page 140).

At present ASK is at the end of Phase 1 of its development. The software is generic and web based in its approach but we intend to develop it further by investigating the feasibility of integrating Web 2.0 functionality. The team were mindful that the wish to add new Web 2.0 functionality needed to be balanced against the success and usability of the current product and any changes/additions must add to the flexibility of ASK without alienating those who prefer a simple approach. Czarnecki's (Anon, 2007) statement that 'we are always in a state of [constant] beta' when using Web 2.0 implies that, by definition, there is no best way to 'Web 2.0' an

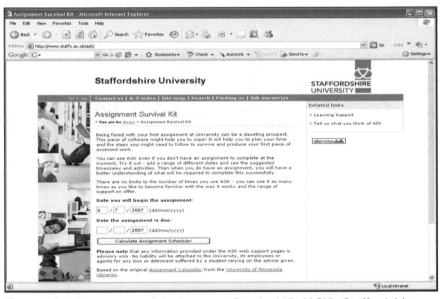

Figure 14.1 Homepage of Assignment Survival Kit (ASK), Staffordshire
University, www.staffs.ac.uk/ask.
Reproduced with thanks by permission of Staffordshire University.

existing application, so the emphasis initially will be on allowing students
to opt in to some of the new functionality, rather than forcing it on them
in its entirety. ASK does, however, already fit with the Web 2.0 philosophy
of openness and sharing and this will be retained in Phase 2 through the
application of a Creative Commons licence.

Phase 1 development pre-Web 2.0

The first task was to agree an appropriate IL structure for ASK which
would meet the needs of SU students. Informed deliberations within the
IL Project Group concluded that IL models have many similarities and few
differences, a view shared by Owusu-Ansah (2003) and Andretta (2005).
This is to some extent unsurprising as many are drawn from the ACRL (ALA)
model (2000) or are a synthesis of a number of existing models. With this
view the IL components used in constructing the ASK stages were drawn
from across existing IL models but principally ANZIIL (Bundy, 2004)
and Big Blue (2002).

Set out below are the ASK framework stages with the corresponding IL
components shown in parentheses:

- Step 1:   Where do I start? (recognizing the information need)
- Step 2:   How do I approach my assignment? (addressing the information need)
- Step 3:   How do I plan my assignment?
- Step 4:   How do I start my research?
- Step 5:   How do I find the books I need? (retrieving the information required)
- Step 6:   How do I find journals?
- Step 7:   Is there any other material I could use?
- Step 8:   How do I use my research? (evaluating the information critically)
- Step 9:   How do I write my assignment up? (adapting the information, organizing and communicating the information)
- Step 10: Have I done all that is required? (reviewing the process)

We accept that IL models are abstract models of the information behaviour process (Hepworth, 2004) and do not necessarily reflect the learning process as described by writers such as Bloom (1956), Kolb, Rubin and Osland (1991), Gibbs, Morgan and Northedge (1998), and Race (2001). In recognition of these issues it is our view that the IL structure embodied in ASK can be regarded as a metacognitive tool that provides a self-regulatory framework for completing assignments. By metacognition we mean an awareness of one's own thinking processes and also the ability to plan, monitor and evaluate that thinking (Moseley et al., 2004). We believe this appears to underpin the iterative process mentioned in many learning theories, information literacy and information behaviour models. Hence the ASK structure provides a thinking skills framework that enables students to complete assignments.

It was our goal to create a tool that would allow students to experience the construction stage of learning, where learners apply new concepts to meaningful tasks, rather than simply convey information. We believe that ASK reaches beyond the inert information-bound web page, defined by Mayes (1995) as 'primary courseware' which is only useful in the conceptualization stage of learning, to that of 'secondary courseware' which enables a learning task, such as completing an assignment, to be carried out.

Creating a deliverable product

ASK results from Information Services' desire to create deliverables to support the information literacy initiative. SU has a fully articulated information literacy policy: the *Information Literacy Statement of Good Practice*, which is formally linked to the University's Learning, Teaching and Assessment Strategy for 2006–9. The development of the software is part of IS's contribution to the University's Widening Participation strategy and demonstrates an enthusiasm to underpin the institution's emphasis on retention.

Aimed at supporting first-year undergraduates but perhaps especially those from non-traditional backgrounds, ASK helps students make the adaptation required to study at a higher level. It encourages the use and raises awareness of the wide range of resources that are available. Once a student enters his or her assignment deadline date, a detailed ten-step schedule (outlined above) mapping out key dates for completion of the work is returned. This schedule gives a suggested timescale for activities, including planning the essay or report, finding and evaluating materials, citing references, writing up and presentation. Figure 14.2 illustrates the first two of these detailed steps.

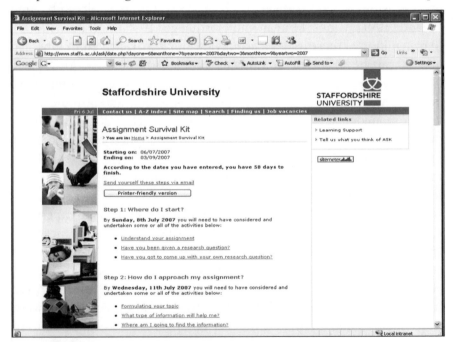

Figure 14.2 Detailed steps page of Assignment Survival Kit (ASK),
Staffordshire University, www.staffs.ac.uk/ask/date.php.
Reproduced with thanks by permission of Staffordshire University.

Feedback and usage

Since going live in mid-October 2006 the software has been positively received by students and academic colleagues. An entire Faculty plans to highlight the software in preparing students to hand in their first piece of written work. A Faculty Director said,

> We used to offer surgery sessions where a member of staff took students through the entire planning process for their assignments. The resource implications were high and we eventually were not able to continue with it. ASK now provides the students with a similar service – only better, since the software can be accessed at any time and as often as needed.

A lecturer said, 'It is particularly useful for mature students because they are terrified of their first assignment; anything to get them started is useful.' One student commented, 'It is much more than a time management tool; it explains how to do research as well. I think it is really useful.' Another said that she 'used it like a diary'.

To assess usage the Sitemeter hit counter (www.sitemeter.com) was added to the site in mid-February 2007. From mid-February to mid-July 2007 there was a total of 1056 separate hits on the site. More detailed analysis of the data indicates that the use of ASK was at a peak in late February, and again in mid- to late March. This corresponds to times when many students receive assignments, e.g. week beginning 19 February, 118 hits, and week beginning 26 March, 95 hits. These figures suggest that ASK is providing a service which is of use to students at the point of need. Statistics also indicate that ASK has been used both early morning and in the evening, when specialized Library support staff are unavailable. The pattern of usage from February to July is shown in Figures 14.3 and 14.4 on page 144.

Despite this demonstrable pattern of usage, feedback was mixed and, in particular, we were mindful of the comments made by the Learning Development and Innovation Adviser on the ASK development team. The feeling was that it was too text-based and constricted by the formality of the standard University web page design. It was thought that it lacked interactivity and there were not enough interesting and imaginative graphics to engage the net generation. In view of these observations we began to think about how we might develop the software further.

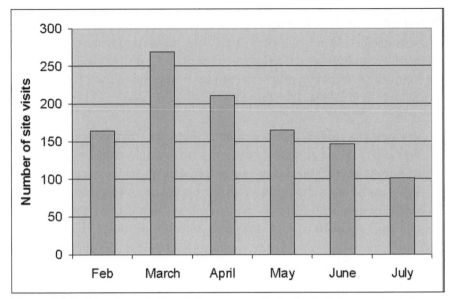

Figure 14.3 Number of site visits per month to ASK, February to July
2007

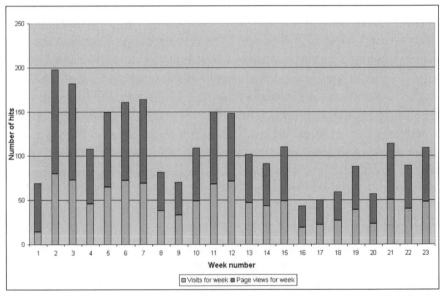

Figure 14.4 Number of visits and page views per week to ASK, February
to July 2007

Web 2.0 development

At present we are looking to develop ASK using Web 2.0 by identifying an appropriate set of features which are relatively easy to add on but which remain student focused. The following are under consideration:

- using Web 2.0 as a participatory platform e.g. RSS feeds
- introducing personalized communications e.g. alerting e-mail, SMS messaging
- introducing portal technology to enhance personalization
- developing the user interface to create more of a recognizable identity
- introducing discipline-specific resources and pathways.

In Phase 2 there are some important new features being developed which fall under the Web 2.0 banner although we do not anticipate including user-generated content because we foresee that we may not at this stage be able to provide a significantly robust quality checking procedure. We are also mindful that many of our users are 'absolute beginners' and they may find content creation challenging. However, these new features include ways in which users' experience of ASK, and the ways they interact with it, can be personalized to meet both their needs and preferences.

One major aspect of Phase 2 will be to look at communicating the information generated by ASK in a way that better allows students to implement the guidelines the software recommends. Currently when students initially use ASK they are restricted to printing off or e-mailing the whole schedule.

Sending 'just in time' reminders through a variety of interfaces would allow students with different preferences to choose the communication method they prefer. It is intended to develop the e-mail feature further, allowing reminders to be sent at key points within the calculated schedule.

The use of SMS and the production of RSS newsfeeds will also be investigated. There are pros and cons to both these technologies: SMS is continuing to grow in popularity (in May 2007 4.5 million texts were sent worldwide; Mobile Data Association, 2007) and almost all students are likely to be existing users, therefore they would not need to learn a new technology and delivery of messages would be timely. There are, however, cost implications with SMS and there is as yet no established solution at SU, although a trial with a selected solution was planned for the end of 2007.

Fewer students may currently be using RSS than SMS – particularly among key target groups – and it does require students to be more proactive in subscribing to an RSS reader. Opgenhaffen (2007) found that RSS is a relatively little used Web 2.0 feature. However, RSS is a growth area as a communication mechanism with many organizations now offering RSS feeds for their news and services. Technically RSS has advantages in being relatively easy to generate, while automating the creation of SMS messages at the appropriate time will be more of a challenge. SMS may be seen more as a social communication method; therefore there are opportunities to harness it for academic purposes. However, students might prefer to compartmentalize their communication: would RSS be viewed as being more appropriate for academic purposes? The student focus group to be set up in 2008 will help inform this debate and possibly become a key driver of new developments.

Students will be able to select whether to receive reminders or not, choose the e-mail address these are delivered to and the mechanism by which the reminders are sent. The development group debated the timing and format of these reminders. It was felt that it may not be appropriate to send reminders at each step, as students may not follow the steps in a fully linear way (Walton et al., 2007), although the schedule provided by ASK does allow them to do this. For example, they may carry out their research using books, the web and journals in parallel, and do this iteratively. Instead it is proposed that reminders are sent when students move to key stages within the assignment framework that correspond to the IL components mentioned earlier. This would occur at the end of 'addressing the information need', 'retrieving information', 'evaluating information' and just before 'organizing/communicating information'.

A number of technologies are being considered to improve both the look and feel and the functionality of ASK. It is proposed that under Phase 2 the whole user interface is reviewed. The solution selected will need to provide a clear identity for ASK and incorporate a wider range of resources, as well as allowing the easy integration of the product within other technological developments at SU.

It is envisaged that ASK will link to a number of other Web 2.0 developments that are taking place locally. For example, a successful trial of subject-specific blogs ran throughout the 2006–7 academic year, and these continue through our e-portfolio system, PebblePAD. Subject wikis are also under development. Our aim is to contribute to a more holistic learning experience and so present the potentially confusing range of resources and systems seamlessly.

Long-term developments for ASK include integration with the SU Student Portal (currently in its pilot phase). Project managers are keen to make ASK available through the portal. This would allow easier personalization for award-specific information and allow the targeting of RSS newsfeeds through existing portlets. Developments within the portal will include personalized calendars enabling the integration of the reminders developed for ASK. When undertaking Phase 2 of ASK, consideration will be given to the most appropriate technology for implementation to allow these longer-term aims to be achieved.

Moving from a generic approach towards an 'end product' approach

ASK in its current format works well and, as shown above, has been well received by users, with its relative simplicity being its 'unique selling point'. It is important to ensure that future developments do not over-complicate it. For this reason, the development team debated the most effective ways in which ASK could develop from the current generic model. In addition to developments mentioned above, it was our intention to enhance the product by making it more appropriate to individual students. We planned to make it possible for students to select their own specific area of study from a range of around twenty different options. An intertwined framework approach using 'hot topics' and reflective learning was successfully tested and used by Bordonaro and Richardson (2004) and this directed us towards the notion that IL support works best when embedded within the students' subject work. In our development meetings, however, we began to look critically at this subject-based approach and to question it. Would the students find this approach helpful in this context?

Our practical experience in supporting students suggested that they might prefer software which guided them through the stages necessary to complete different types of course work, for example, creating a poster, making a presentation or submitting a group portfolio. These were the assignment tasks students were encountering and ASK needed to reflect this diversity and support students as they tried to make use of their research and, importantly, communicate it in a way that was fit for their particular purpose. Although the 'retrieving the information required' component of the IL models may be the same (or very similar) for each assessment type, evaluating and selecting information and then communicating this effectively could be quite different. Using and communicating information for a particular context and purpose is an aspect of IL where many students do not have well developed skills. Adopting this approach will allow us to integrate a wider range of skills, including IT and personal development skills, into the ASK framework, while still allowing further subject context to be added by tutors within a specific module if required. At the time of writing the development team are creating models which show the various steps in travelling along different pathways to complete a variety of assignments. Following these developments we will collect feedback which examines whether the design decisions made were successful for our student constituency.

Conclusion: impact on the HE community

Analysis of Sitemeter statistics shows that the software has been used across the globe. Detailed usage patterns vary over time, although predominant use, as would be expected, has consistently been within SU. Analysis of the results in July 2007 showed that 60% of the use in the last 100 days originated from Staffordshire University.

The ASK site has also been accessed from other UK academic institutions (9%) and from a range of ISPs (28%). It is not possible to identify if the ISP hits are from SU students accessing the system from home or if these users are from elsewhere.

Statistics show 89% of users were from within the UK, with 11% from overseas. Some overseas use may be from colleges abroad where SU has franchises and the students have been specifically introduced to ASK. For others the assumption is that the site is found via a search engine.

These usage figures appear to indicate that ASK can be applied in a number of educational contexts and provides a framework for the application of IL concepts that students can fit to their own individual situation and study needs. We have already received many requests from other institutions to make links to the ASK software and have applied a Creative Commons licence to the software. Winning the CILIP UC&R Award for Innovation has publicized our student support software in a very positive way and the prize money means that our future development work now has some funding. We hope that after local launch in October 2007 we will be able to place the finished product on Jorum so other institutions and their students might benefit.

Developing ASK and then quickly afterwards using Web 2.0 to upgrade its functionality has been a steep learning curve for the team. We have tried very hard not to jump onto the bandwagon of using Web 2.0 developments to 'enhance' the product unless it was truly felt that these additions would contribute to the usefulness of the software for the student users. We have attempted to keep the student perspective, as sometimes it is all too easy to overload a piece of software with improvements that are ultimately technology rather than end-user driven. Most good ideas are simple ones and the development team has been mindful of this in seeking to incorporate additional functionality into ASK. The real challenge now comes not in integrating Web 2.0 but in handling the next, as yet unknown, generation of technological advances in a meaningful and user-friendly way.

References

Andretta, S. (2005) *Information Literacy: a practitioner's guide,* Chandos.

Anon (2007) Constant Beta. Kelly Czarnecki, Public Library of Charlotte & Mecklenburg County, *Library Journal,* (March), www.libraryjournal.com/article/CA6423427.html.

Association of College and Research Libraries (2000) *Information Literacy Competency Standards for Higher Education,* www.ala.org/ala/acrl/acrlstandards/informationliteracycompetency.htm.

Big Blue Project (2002) *The Big Blue: information skills for students. Final report,* www.leeds.ac.uk/bigblue/finalreport.html.

Bloom, B. (1956) *Taxonomy of Educational Objectives Handbook 1: Cognitive Domain,* McGraw-Hill.

Bordonaro, K. and Richardson, G. (2004) Scaffolding and Reflection in Course-integrated Library Instruction, *Journal of Academic Librarianship,* **30** (5), 391–401.

Bundy, A. (2004) *Australian and New Zealand Information Literacy (ANZIIL) Framework: principles, standards and practice,* Adelaide: Australian and New Zealand Institute for Information Literacy, www.anziil.org/resources/Info%20lit%202nd%20edition.pdf.

Gibbs, G., Morgan, A. and Northedge, A. (1998) *Teaching in Higher Education: theory and evidence.* Chapter 6: How Students Learn, Open University.

Hepworth, M. (2004) A Framework for Understanding User Requirements for an Information Service: defining the needs of informal carers, *Journal of the American Society of Information Science and Technology*, **55** (8), 695–708.

Kolb, D. A., Rubin, I. M. and Osland, J. (1991) *Organizational Behavior: an experiential approach,* 5th edn, N. J., Prentice-Hall.

Mayes, J. T. (1995) Learning Technology and Groundhog Day. In Strang, W., Simpson, V. B. and Slater, J. (eds), *Hypermedia at Work: practice and theory in higher education,* University of Kent Press.

Mobile Data Association (2007) *Text it: the UK's definitive text related information source,* www.text.it/mediacentre/sms_figures.cfm.

Moseley, D., Baumfield, V., Higgins, S., Lin, M., Miller, J., Newton, D., Robson, S., Elliott, J. and Gregson, M. (2004) *Thinking Skills Frameworks for Post-16 Learners: an evaluation. A Research Report for the Learning & Skills Research Centre,* Cromwell Press.

Opgenhaffen, M. (2007) Online Journalism and Interactivity: studying control, conversation and self-production from a cognitive and methodological approach. Paper given at the *Information, Interactions and Impact Conference,* Robert Gordon University June 25–28, 2007.

Owusu-Ansah, E. K. (2003) Information Literacy and the Academic Library: a critical look at a concept and the controversies surrounding it, *Journal of Academic Librarianship*, **29** (4), 219–30.

Race, P. (2001) *The Lecturer's Toolkit: a resource for developing learning, teaching and assessment,* 2nd edn, Kogan Page.

Walton, G., Barker, J., Hepworth, M. and Stephens, D. (2007) Using Online Collaborative Learning to Enhance Information Literacy Delivery in a Level 1 Module: an evaluation, *Journal of Information Literacy*, **1** (1), 13–30.

Part 4

The future

Chapter 15

Teaching information literacy through digital games

JOHN KIRRIEMUIR

Introduction

As new formats have become available over the last century, libraries have gradually widened the range of media they hold. In addition to books, magazines and newspapers, many public libraries now hold CDs, DVDs, cassettes and videos. It is therefore not surprising that one of the newest, but widely marketed, forms of entertainment media – computer and video games – is appearing on the shelves of some public libraries, with librarians such as Scalzo (2006) successfully operating video game loaning schemes.

However, it isn't just in lending that video games are used within the library sector. Neiburger (2007a) and others have run video gaming events, workshops and tournaments within their buildings. National libraries are involved; since 1992, every video game distributed in France must have two copies deposited in the Bibliothèque Nationale de France, the French national library. An increasing number of conferences, such as the ALA TechSource Gaming, Learning, and Libraries Symposium (ALA, 2007), are dedicated to analysing the ways in which video games can be used by the library sector.

Computer and video games and simulations are increasingly central to training and teaching, especially in the business, health, education and military sectors. However, their application to education in libraries has so far been negligible. One potential use for such games in this sector has been in the teaching and reinforcement of information literacy skills. This chapter examines some aspects of computer games which make them potential tools for instruction in this subject domain, and concludes with details of three ongoing projects to develop video games for the acquisition of such skills.

Digital games

How popular are video games? In short – very. Games console sales are measured in tens of millions, for example the Nintendo Gameboy series (200 million) and the Sony Playstation 2 (120 million). Sales of titles such as The Sims (16 million), Nintendogs (15 million) and Tetris (33 million) are comparable in magnitude to those of popular book franchises, such as Harry Potter. In the first day of release, Halo 3 for the Xbox 360 earned $170 million; as the BBC (2007) pointed out, 'The game sets the record for the most money earned in a day by an entertainment product, topping figures set by the film Spiderman 3.'

Despite the popularity of what is a mainstream form of entertainment, most populist articles concerning video games focus on negative aspects of this medium, with article titles such as 'Why Computer Games Should Worry Parents' (Bantick, 2004). The stereotypical image of video game players, for example, is of a teenage boy, playing violent games in social isolation in his bedroom. It is a peculiarity that many of these 'negative aspects', such as the sedentary nature of gameplay and a lack of social contact when playing, could equally be applied to the act of reading a book, or watching television. However, as in the early days of cinema and its vocal opponents, so video games are, as a relatively new entertainment medium, subject to such critique.

Three aspects of the video game culture in particular predominate in the reporting media. It is wise for librarians intending to use video games to read about these and other issues concerning games so as to be informed when discussing with peers, parents and funders.

Violence

This is the most contentious issue concerning games, perhaps not surprisingly considering the increasing 'realism' and that children form a considerable minority of game players. Several commentators, such as Thomson (2005), point out that many studies and literature reviews on this topic present contradictory findings. Other research conflicts, stating that violent video games may not affect many people, or may provide a useful and harmless outlet for various emotions, or may provide a catalyst to further violent actions.

It surprises many people to learn that violent games form only a minority of commercially available titles and, like films, operate under a classification system. Neiburger (2007a) points out that only 15% of the games sold in the USA in 2005 were rated M (Mature), while 53% were rated E (for everyone) or E-10+ (for ages 10 and up).

Demographic

Digital game players are not predominantly teenage boys. Several studies e.g. CNN (2004), indicate that the largest demographic of such players is middle-aged women, while a growing body of news reports, e.g. Borland (2007), indicate that the more physical Nintendo Wii is being used by the elderly in institutions such as retirement homes. As many first and second generation game players carry on their leisure activity into adult life and parenthood, so the average age of players creeps up; various estimates such as Entertainment Software Association (2007) put this figure in the early to mid-thirties. Women make up a sizeable proportion of these, with estimates for the proportion of female video and online game players being around 40%.

Social contact and stimulation

Linked to the argument of violence is the social isolation of game players, as discussed by researchers such as Thompson (2002) and, in detail, by Cover (2006). The reality is the opposite: most games feature a multiplayer option, and all consoles have the facility for several people to play at once. Popular titles, such as Halo and Mario Kart, are developed more towards group or online social play rather than single player capability. Research points to game players having an above-average grasp of social awareness and responsibility; for example, Neiburger (2007b) points out that 73% of gamers vote in elections. Among parents who play video games, the Entertainment Software Association (2007) reports that 80% play video games with their children, spending 9.1 hours a month playing games as a family.

Several authors of books analysing digital game play, for example Gee (2003) and Johnson (2005), discuss the large quantity of information the player has to rapidly absorb (in several formats such as sound, text, graphics, feedback to input), evaluate, process and manipulate. It is this particular observation that has generated considerable interest in studying the role of digital games in learning.

Digital games in learning

Games have been an integral part of learning activities in many civilizations. Crawford (1982) observed that:

> Games are . . . the most ancient and time honoured vehicle for education. They are the original educational technology, the natural one, having received the seal of approval of natural selection. We don't see mother lions lecturing cubs at the chalkboard; we don't see senior lions writing their memoirs for posterity. In light of this, the question, 'Can games have educational value?' becomes absurd.

Throughout our education, games are used in different forms to help us learn and retain content, and to develop and improve skills. Games are especially used to 'learn the basics' in primary schooling, such as the alphabet and numbers, while the increasing use of digital media for adult language learning often incorporates game-based memorization and testing.

Levine (2006) summarizes six attributes of game use through history:

- games test our problem-solving skills
- games are inclusive
- games create community
- games facilitate learning
- games provide fields for practice of leadership and team skills
- games develop identity.

The use of games in learning has been studied for several decades; in the last century, such studies were usually confined to the psychology and sociology disciplines. A number of studies from this research body (Jones, 1997; Mumtaz, 2000; Turkle, 1984) discussed some of the positive educational attributes of the emerging medium of digital games.

However, the last decade has seen a growing interest in the learning, educational and teaching uses of digital games as part of a cross-subject discipline involving cognitive science, pedagogy theory, and psychology and media science. Most of this interest has focused on the application of games to childhood learning. For example, research evidence indicates that, through processes of discussion, collaboration and reflection on games embedded in peer-group cultures, children learn how to play, and perhaps learn, in collaboration with others (Williamson and Facer, 2003).

However, some of the more recent research focuses less on particular demographics and more on the processes involved in digital game use. For example, Squire and Steinkuehler (2005) demonstrate that playing the online game Lineage involves considerable amounts of writing, research, the development of maps, and an understanding of currencies and micro-economics. The research aspect is of particular interest: 'Research is a core component of game play. Gamers find and interpret data to determine where the best hunting is, for example. They also publish results through game forums (official sources) and clan forums (unofficial sources) and build spreadsheet models to compare the effectiveness of strategies.'

Most digital games have some degree of simulation within, whether it is of the recognizable, such as operating a theme park or being mayor of a city, or the fantastical, for example flying a dragon. Dumbleton and Kirriemuir (2006) summarize four benefits, and three drawbacks, of the use of digital gaming simulations in many educational, business and training applications:

1 Results (the 'effect') from trying a particular strategy can be obtained quickly, therefore providing feedback on the outcome of a particular strategy.
2 Simulations can be re-run, often quickly, with various factor changes to view alternative outcomes.
3 Scenarios can be developed by a facilitator for repeated, use e.g. by a teacher for use in group analysis work.
4 In scientific simulations, such as the mixing of chemicals to view reactions, there is no cost, mess or (in these litigious times) danger involved.
5 Scenario complexity is bound to the complexity of the game. The number of variables that the player can alter in a game is limited (McFarlane and Sakellariou, 2002) and often does not reflect the randomness and complexity of 'real life'.

6   Also, chance and luck, and factors that are immeasurable and for all intents take on the attributes of chance, are infrequently programmed into games or are provided in an explicit, limited manner.
7   Video games and simulations are not a total replacement for 'real life' training; for example, no matter how realistic a medical or surgery training game is, at some point the surgeon is going to have to cut through real flesh into a real human being.

Gee (2003) describes a scenario-exploration process for most video gameplay, not just those games which are more overtly simulation in nature. From an information perspective, his process consists of a four-stage cycle:

1   The player probes the virtual world.
2   Based on the results of the probe, the player forms a hypothesis about what something – such as a text, object, artefact, event or action – might mean in a useful way.
3   The player re-probes the world, using the hypothesis as the basis of their actions.
4   The player treats the resulting effect as feedback.

Various researchers (Inkpen et al., 1995; Higgins, 2000; Whitebread, 1997) have suggested that games that encourage this form of iterative probing can support the development of logical thinking and problem solving, important in learning information literacy skills.

Digital games to teach information literacy

In 2001 more than 30% of US academic libraries offered information literacy credit courses. Unfortunately, studies found that students ranked credit courses as their least preferred means of getting library instruction, compared with individual instruction conducted at the point of need while students are actively seeking information (Davidson, 2001).

There is no clear agreement on why such courses receive a negative preference. The body of research into applied education to contemporary school and academic classes gives a wide range of potential reasons. One of the most frequently cited is that as a result of growing up with a wider array of easily accessible media, contemporary students are accustomed to being continually entertained, or motivated for longer periods, and this has shaped their expectations for more engaging instruction (Soloway, 1991). Traditional methods of delivering credit courses are possibly less likely to engage or stimulate students to a level where they are receptive, attentive and absorbing content within an appropriate context.

Levine (2006) concludes the introduction of her Library Technology report with: 'How long until someone develops a professional, compelling game that teaches information literacy? My estimation, "Not long."'

This is not surprising. The academic library and education sectors are intrinsically linked. Many librarians, themselves first or second generation gamers, are aware of the increasing use of computer and video games in the university, college and school sectors. And, like academic staff, librarians are increasingly aware of the digital media and video game-based culture in which many of their patrons are immersed. It is natural, therefore, for the library sector to consider the use of video games within its own teaching domain. To enhance information literacy instruction, librarians such as Michelle Boule (2007) consider that:

> We [librarians] could also build games that teach information literacy. If a game were to present a problem to users, sending them down the path of information gathering, various kinds of information could be presented. The player might have to choose between scholarly and popular sources, information formats, and then synthesize the information into useable answers to the problem.

Branston (2006) reminds us that another reason the video game is potentially an excellent framework to teach information literacy skills has to do with the fact that many game players often partake in secondary research to assist them in their game play. This involves the use of walkthroughs, cheats, FAQs, guides (in printed form and online), and exchanging information with their peers.

Consequently, it comes as little surprise that several information literacy projects, which involve the design and use of digital games as a core component, are at various stages of development in higher education. We will now examine three such initiatives in more detail.

University of North Texas

The University of North Texas Library is developing an online educational game to teach information literacy to its students. The learning outcomes of the game will be based on the ACRL Information Literacy Competency Standards for Higher Education (2000). The game takes a holistic view of information literacy (Downey and Boyett, 2007), defining it as '... much more than just being able to do research. IL involves being able to develop research questions, knowing how and where to look for answers, and requires that students understand legal and ethical issues of information use.'

The game is a first-person character-driven environment, the player solving problems to proceed in a linear way to the next of 16 modules. The substantial size of the game necessitates the inclusion of a 'save game' facility, while functionality to allow teachers and librarians to monitor progress is also being included.

Students who have completed the 16-module game will be compared to students who have received information literacy instruction through other formats to determine if improved learning occurred through use of the game. This will, of course, be of great interest to libraries interested in developing similar games, and the games-in-learning research community.

University of North Carolina

The game being created by this university library uses a question-and-answer format, allowing two to four students to play against each other by answering questions about information literacy. Topics are taken from categories such as 'Choose your Resource', 'Avoiding Plagiarism' and 'Searching and Using Databases'.

The game also has a one-player version in which students provide timed responses to questions. In addition to the four categories, special squares on a Trivial Pursuit-like board ask students to find a specific piece of information on an actual website, or to compare two websites based on specific criteria, such as authority or currency.

From the perspective of information literacy (Harris and Rice, 2007) the game has five objectives, namely that by completion students will:

• understand that information can be found in a variety of sources and will recognize how that understanding can help determine the direction of a search for specific information

- understand the importance of the organizational content, bibliographic structure, function and use of information sources
- identify useful information from the library's catalogue, online journal indexes and other information systems
- understand the way collections of information sources are organized and accessed
- properly and appropriately cite sources.

In late 2007, the game will be marketed to first-year instructors and publicized directly to students through Facebook, the library website and Blackboard, the networked course management system. The game can also be freely downloaded and reconfigured, with their own content, by other libraries; the developers maintain a blog (Library Games, 2007) providing news of game development and adaptations.

Arizona State University

An ongoing project at the Fletcher Library in Arizona State University (www.west.asu.edu/libcontrib/game/website) is designed to improve information and library skills among first-year students. The project initially started by developing a board game, the resulting trials of which were positive. Three later stages of the project development plan involve:

- designing a computer game that would simulate the complex processes of selecting, using and evaluating multiple sources of information within a library setting
- aligning the concepts taught within the game to the curriculum and the institution's Information Skills Outcomes for First-Year Students plan
- designing a computer game that would incorporate assessment of student learning, providing students with immediate, automatic feedback of their actions and skill level.

Development of the game began in January 2006, and involved hiring game programmers, with the intended product being Flash-based. Allgood (2006) outlines the development process, which follows that of professional commercial games (though with only a fraction of the budget), including storyline development, character interaction development, sound creation, bug tracking and documentation.

Conclusion

Despite the sniping of modern-day Luddites and cultural elitists within the media, video games are here to stay. The medium has been commercially successful for over 30 years, a significant proportion of the population spend considerable time and personal money enjoying its use, and players are increasingly spread across all demographics and age groups. Consequently, a significant and increasing proportion of library patrons are active gamers, familiar and comfortable with video games and gaining transferable skills through their play.

Information literacy is not an easy subject to teach students, especially those who study in domains requiring little contact with, and use of, technology. If anything, the contemporary net-based world makes the point of acquiring these skills more obscure, as many people are stuck in a 'Google-and-go' mentality. The growing diversity and complexity of information sources, and issues such as information quality and citation, make information literacy an increasingly complex set of skills to gain – but, for those reasons, a more crucial set than ever to acquire.

It seems natural, therefore, to look for new tools that make use of our overtly digital culture, to see if they can support this teaching domain. Computer and video games, as successfully used in other domains, may be able to play a useful role. The evaluation of the three projects described in the previous section, and any similar projects, will provide valuable information to others in the library sector considering using digital games to support information literacy development.

References

ALA (2007) *ALA TechSource Gaming, Learning, and Libraries Symposium,* Chicago, USA, July 2007, http://gaming.techsource.ala.org.

Allgood, T. (2006) Game On! Developing a Game for Library Instruction, *Internet Librarian Conference,* Monterey, California, USA, 25 October 2006.

Association of College and Research Libraries (2000) *Information Literacy Competency Standards for Higher Education,* www.ala.org/ala/acrl/acrlstandards/informationliteracycompetency.htm.

Bantick, C. (2004) Why Computer Games should Worry Parents, *The Age,* 15 January.

BBC (2007) *Halo 3 sales top £84m in 24 hours,* 27 September, http://news.bbc.co.uk/1/hi/technology/7015663.stm.

Borland, S. (2007) Elderly 'Addicted' to Nintendo Wii at Care Home, *Daily Telegraph*, 14 September, www.telegraph.co.uk/news/main.jhtml?xml=/news/2007/09/14/ngame114.xml.

Boule, M. (2007) Serious Games, *Association of College and Research Libraries* (blog), http://acrlblog.org/2007/06/06/serious-games.

Branston, C. (2006) From Game Studies to Bibliographic Gaming: libraries tap into the video game culture, *Bulletin of the American Society for Information Science and Technology*, **32** (4), 24-9.

Cover, R. (2006) Gaming (Ad)diction: discourse, identity, time and play in the production of the gamer addiction myth, *Game Studies*, **6** (1), http://gamestudies.org/0601/articles/cover.

CNN (2004) *Study: women over 40 biggest online gamers*, http://edition.cnn.com/2004/TECH/fun.games/02/11/video.games.women.reut.

Crawford, C. (1982) *The Art of Computer Game Design*. Out of print: available online at www.vancouver.wsu.edu/fac/peabody/game-book/Coverpage.html.

Davidson, J. R. (2001) Faculty and Student Attitudes Toward Credit Course for Library Skills, *College and Research Libraries*, **62** (2), 155-63.

Downey, A. and Boyett, K. (2007) Information Literacy through Unique Education Gaming Application, *American Library Association TechSource Gaming, Learning, and Libraries Symposium*, Chicago, USA, 2007.

Dumbleton, T. and Kirriemuir, J. (2006) Digital Games and Education. In Rutter, J. and Bryce, J. (eds), *Understanding Digital Games*, SAGE Publications.

Entertainment Software Association (2007) *Game Player Data* www.theesa.com/facts/gamer_data.php.

Gee, J. P. (2003) *What Video Games Have to Teach Us about Learning and Literacy*, Palgrave Macmillan.

Harris, A. and Rice, S. (2007) Games Students Play: a new approach to online information literacy instruction, *American Library Association TechSource Gaming, Learning, and Libraries Symposium*, Chicago, USA, 2007.

Higgins, S. (2000) The Logical Zoombinis, *Teaching Thinking*, **1** (1).

Inkpen, K. M., Booth, K. S., Gribble, S. D. and Klawe, M. M. (1995) Give and Take: children collaborating on one computer. In Bowers, J. M. and Benford, S. D. (eds), *CHI 95: Human Factors in Computing Systems*, Denver, CO, ACM Conference Companion, 258-9.

Johnson, S. (2005) *Everything Bad Is Good for You: how today's popular culture is actually making us smarter*, Riverhead Books.

Jones, M.G. (1997) Learning to Play; Playing to Learn: lessons learned from computer games, *Association for Educational Communications and Technology Conference*, Albuquerque, USA, 1997, www.gsu.edu/~wwwitr/docs/mjgames.

Levine, J. (2006) *Gaming and Libraries: intersection of services*, **42** (5), Library Technology Reports, American Library Association.

Library Games (2007) *University of North Carolina Library Games Project* (blog), http://librarygames.blogspot.com.

McFarlane, A. and Sakellariou, S. (2002) The Role of ICT in Science Education, *Cambridge Journal of Education*, **32** (2), 219-32.

Mumtaz, S. (2000) *Using ICT in Schools: a review of the literature on learning, teaching and software evaluation*, Centre for New Technologies Research in Education, University of Warwick.

Neiburger, E. (2007a) *Gamers . . . in the Library?!*, American Library Association.

Neiburger, E. (2007b) The Payoff, Up Close and Personal, *American Library Association TechSource Gaming, Learning, and Libraries Symposium*, Chicago, USA, 2007.

Scalzo, J. (2006) The Video Game Librarian: it's the end of the year as we know it (and I feel fine), *Gaming Target* (25 January), www.gamingtarget.com/article.php?artid=4941.

Soloway, E. (1991) How the Nintendo Generation Learns, *Communications of the ACM,* **34**, 23-8.

Squire, L. and Steinkuehler, C. (2005) Meet the Gamers, *Library Journal* (15 April), www.libraryjournal.com/article/CA516033.html.

Thompson, C. (2002) Violence and the Political Life of Videogames. In King, L. (ed.), *Game On: the history and culture of videogames*, Universe Publishing.

Thomson, I. (2005) *Conflict Reigns Over Violent Gaming Aggression*, www.vnunet.com/vnunet/news/2141383/jury-violent-games.

Turkle, S. (1984) *The Second Self: computers and the human spirit*, Simon & Schuster.

Whitebread, D. (1997) Developing Children's Problem-solving: the educational uses of adventure games. In McFarlane, A. (ed.), *Information Technology and Authentic Learning*, Routledge.

Williamson, B. and Facer, K. (2003) *More Than 'Just a Game': the implications for schools of childrens' computer games communities*, unpublished draft paper.

Chapter 16

Conclusion

PETER GODWIN

Is Library 2.0 dead? The cynics may say that it never really had a life of its own. Others may be saying that it has peaked. Maybe the usefulness of the title 'Library 2.0' has passed. What is more certain is that the spirit is still present, and we should take Bradley's advice (2007) to 'forget the 2.0 label and consider how you can do things better'. Following the original ethos, the mainstream libraries will take what they want from the movement. The 2.0 mentality is here to stay. There is no going back: only further future developments, into a new 3D web and searching into David Weinberger's (2007) 'kind of' world. In this concluding chapter we will take a look at how Web 2.0 is shaping the world we live in, the operation of the most significant 2.0 tools for the delivery of IL, followed by new technological developments, and how this affects the IL mission.

Our changing 2.0 world

Andrew Keen admits that his book *The Cult of the Amateur: how today's internet is killing our culture* (2007) is a polemic. He lampoons the untrustworthiness of sites like Wikipedia, YouTube, Google and MySpace. He loathes the way in which anyone can now post their opinions via blogs, however extreme or poorly written. This activity implies that unqualified public opinion is equal to that of experts. In this 2.0 world people are becoming accustomed to getting items for free, which undermines paid expertise, and further diminishes the respect for intellectual property. The web generation can seem threatening: how far should academics and librarians give them the kind of experience that we think they want, and pander to their gadgetry? Michael Gorman (2007), former President of the American Library Association, has been a vocal critic of what he calls the 'Blog people', and of the adoption of 2.0 technologies. He also decries the digital Maoism which devalues expert opinion and raises up the wisdom of the crowd. Surely we, as library professionals, should point out that experts are not always right and that we can all learn through dialogue with peers and a variety of resources. We are going to have to accept user tagging in our catalogues and these entries will supplement, not destroy, our catalogue entries. The co-existence of amateur with professional is something that we should both understand and promote. This can only enhance our IL mission.

Despite the venom, Keen knows there is no retreat. It is with his indicators of what the future holds that we can identify. He says, on behalf of his children: 'we need more media literacy in class. What we read on Wikipedia is not necessarily true, but kids assume that what they read on the internet is true. I think there needs to be some serious studies. Researchers have to go out and ask kids "When you read a blog, do you think it's true?"' (Keen, 2007). So whether we take on board all his strictures or not, Andrew Keen and his ilk are our allies.

We could agree that Citizendium (http://en.citizendium.org/wiki) is a project worth encouraging. This kind of peer-reviewed Wikipedia was launched in September 2006 as 'an experimental new wiki project that combines public participation with gentle expert guidance', according to Larry Sanger, its founder (Sanger, 2007). Progress has been slow, if deliberate, and in March 2007 there were only about 1100 live articles. It is a service to watch. Some newspapers are managing to combine their professional content with amateur content in associated blogs. *Guardian Unlimited* (www.guardian.co.uk) is a notable example of this. In other words, news sites have gone social: 96% of newspaper websites in the USA have RSS feeds, 5% offer at least one reporter blog, and 33% now allow comments on articles (Bivings Group, 2007). Rumours are circulating that the *Wall Street Journal* may become available free online (McIntyre, 2007), which may precipitate a domino effect with other publications. The dynamics of newspaper delivery are therefore evolving along with comment on their content.

It is the web generation learners who are likely to be most attracted to these developments. Joan Lippincott (2006) emphasizes the experiential and active side of web learners, the use of gaming, taking polls of opinions and encouragement to create content. Michael Furdyk may have summarized the characteristics of our web generation learners best in the ACEL/ASCD Conference in Australia, October 2007 (O'Connell, 2007) as 'multiprocessing; multimedia literacy; discovery-based learning; bias towards action; staying connected; zero tolerance for delays; consumer/creator blurring; social networking'. Barnes, Marateo and Ferris (2007) confirm that social networking tools being used by the web generation students have great potential for teaching them how to learn.

However, reflecting on the tools like blogs, podcasting, YouTube and wikis, we should not be lured into believing they are the answer to reinvigorating education or to renovating our libraries. Kids are not all going to become great writers as a result of blogging. Not everyone is good at writing a reflective blog and not everyone will bother to listen to a podcast even if they subscribe in the first place. These media are not intrinsically powerful. Their difference lies in the possibility of taking part in a bigger production, with the chance of a worldwide audience (Guhlin, 2007). This can have its appeal, and is attached to the concept of the so-called wisdom of the crowd. It is too early to say how quickly this novelty will wear off.

Librarians' response to Web 2.0

Librarians are responding dramatically to Library 2.0.and we can be forgiven for thinking that we wanted Library 2.0 library services and have got Library 2.0 librarians instead (Deschamps, 2007). The US public library sector in particular is leaping ahead (Houghton-John, 2007a). For example, the Harris County Public Library, Texas, is seeking in its programme (begun August 2007) to introduce its users to the Web 2.0 technologies, which 'are reshaping the context of information on the internet today' (http://ihcpl2.blogspot.com/2007/08/about-ihcpl-program.html). This staff programme, based on the Charlotte and Mecklenburg programme, has now been opened up to the public. The state of Victoria planned to begin a Learning 2.0 programme for over 1000 library workers in October 2007 based on the same programme (Abram, 2007). The importance of beginning to become familiar with Web 2.0 technologies is therefore great for librarians in all sectors. Formal training courses can play a part, but it is characteristic of the tools that they are open source and should not require long courses: in other words, they can be explored and the basics gained through individual effort. This is a trend which will continue and is aided by blog posts such as '10 ways to find time for 23 Things' (Greenhill, 2007). Another notable example is from Saskatchewan, Canada: 'Meet the Stars: Books and Web 2.0' (http://disruptiveinnovators.wikispaces.com/Books+%26+Web+2), an online professional development course for local teacher-librarians, which champions the use of Web 2.0 in classrooms and school libraries and is an example of good practice.

Web 2.0 and information literacy

As librarians become conversant with the Web 2.0 tools, they have to decide where they fit in relation to IL teaching. There are those that increase the subject content available to students (e.g. Wikipedia), those that can be used to deliver IL (e.g. blogs, YouTube) and those that will help students to become more proficient learners. Many of these have great potential for distance learners or for blended learning (Secker, 2007). What is our role in telling students about the best web applications for their study? This can range from Google Documents through Yahoo! Notepad, Pageflakes, Gliffy, Wikipedia, Google News, Facebook, Google Calendar, Calcoolate, to Zotero (Catone, 2007). It is in the use of these developing technologies to discover and use information that we should make our contribution. The major difference between these and previous applications is that they are freely available on the web and can be used and applied without huge amounts of training, i.e. through individual effort and initiative. In our IL delivery we may therefore be encouraging the use of a variety of Web 2.0 tools to assist the student research process. The student who is going to make most effective use of the information should consider use of a personalized start page like Netvibes, Pageflakes or iGoogle; use of an RSS feed aggregator like Bloglines; a social bookmarking system like del.icio.us, and referencing systems like Zotero.

We shall now review the major tools and how they impact on IL.

Blogs and wikis

Blogs will be powerful for a variety of reasons, including:

- The opportunities they give librarians in all types of education, particularly HE, for working collaboratively with teachers, building mutual respect and helping to embed IL into the curriculum, where it belongs, as part of the disciplinary discourse, rather than some adjunct.
- The fact that blogging encourages creative writing in many pupils, and librarians can assist by providing material to encourage creativity.
- The potential of reaching and sharing information with a worldwide audience, facilitating distance learning in particular.
- The attraction of keeping a log and reflecting on the research process.
- The opportunity given to librarians to be able to have a dialogue with a class of students and support their research process, long after the initial one or two project sessions.
- The importance of the blogosphere as an information source for latest news, opinion and discourse between experts.

Wikipedia is both a powerful information source and an instrument to deliver all kinds of IL messages. It will be recommended by librarians as a starting point for users to find quick information about a topic. Verification against other sources will be recommended. Tuition could then include showing how easily data can be entered, how to track how it got there through the 'history' facility, and the usefulness of reference lists at the foot of entries. Wikipedia could also be used to help students distinguish between fact and opinion and therefore aid the development of their critical thinking skills. Perhaps most significant of all will be the use made of hyperlinks in entries which will lead researchers to all manner of unexpected discoveries. Wikipedia's coverage will continue to grow and the ease of use will ensure its popularity.

The wiki will have a variety of future uses for IL delivery. The recent availability of Wetpaint, the popular wiki software, as an adjunct on Facebook may encourage the use of wikis by librarians as a practical alternative to use of wikis within VLEs.

For example, we may find wikis:

- in IL to encourage building a list of resources or collaborating on a group project
- in units to deliver IL, e.g. LRS 590: Beyond Google at Pratt University (http://beyondgoogle.pbwiki.com/)

- as containers for a subject guide, e.g. 'The Business Library', a comprehensive business subject guide run by Chad Boeninger at Ohio State University (www.library.ohiou.edu/subjects/bizwiki/index.php/Main_Page)
- being used by librarians to share their instruction good practice, e.g. the Oregon Library Instruction Wiki (http://instructionwiki.org/Main_Page).

Quick communication: RSS and IM

Instant messaging systems (IM) as used at Cameron Library, University of Alberta, may set a trend. There it is used as an alerting mechanism, to communicate to library staff the need for individual help. This leads to a visit to the workstation or laptop wherever the person is situated (Houghton-John, 2007b).

RSS feeds are like the glue that binds together 2.0 services, and will increasingly become the main means by which serious researchers will gather together their current material from blogs, news alerting services and database searches. Librarian-created subject pages could be converted into RSS feeds, possibly with the addition of subject tags to increase access.

Reaching and entertaining: YouTube, podcasting and Second Life

YouTube has become a fantastic resource for locating short videos which may be useful in helping students learn a technique or as a teaching springboard to provoke discussion, e.g. 'Shift Happens Narrated' (for discussion on globalization, www.youtube.com/watch?v=FqfunyCeU5g); 'Scholarly versus Popular Periodicals' (for demonstrating the differences, http://uk.youtube.com/watch?v=VeyR30Yq1tA); 'Where Do I Begin? Compendex!' (for introducing this database, www.youtube.com/watch?v=4L6UATvaj5A).

Podcasting allows easy creation of audio content to reach the selected target, and a distribution akin to allowing your customers to set up a bank standing order. However, it has no inherent value (Carnegie Mellon University, 2007) but may be used to help librarians to reach their goals via a channel that appeals to some users. A major limitation lies in the impossibility of dialogue between client and podcaster, and because of this, usage is only going to appeal to a minority and promotion will have to be heavy. Curtin University Library in Australia is an outstanding example of an academic library which has embraced the medium, producing podcasts at introductory and advanced level, as well as book reviews and 'Opinion', a vehicle for making comments and discussion on library services.

Second Life (SL) is the virtual world where we can participate and create our own surroundings and objects. It is both exciting and puzzling. How can such a 'place' exist with an economy, yet reside only as the front end of a number of application servers on the internet? The strangeness of the whole enterprise will repel some, fascinate others and make a few very rich! It is not a game, because there are no clear goals or winners (Grassian and Truman, 2007). Its attraction is that it provides a situation which gives the space and opportunity for anyone to interact on a level playing field on equal terms, like another one of Tom Friedman's flattening phenomena brought about by technology (Grassian and Truman, 2007). Another way of looking at it is to see the other Web 2.0 tools discussed as words and pages; SL lifts you from your chair and makes you interact in a virtual world via your avatar, who becomes 'you' (Nino, 2007). From a library point of view, SL gives the opportunity for avatars to have a real-life kind of exchange and get the feeling of personal contact that is not present in e-mail or IM. Libraries may opt to produce videos (minima) and chatbots (reference question responses) as part of their IL armoury (Grassian and Truman, 2007). An example of a librarian working with faculty to utilize SL can be found in Denyse Rodriguez, who created an SL course for a fourth-year Employee Relations course at Mount St Vincent University in Canada (WILU, 2007). The use of these virtual worlds could connect through from the local VLE or with e-learning sites.

How far students will react favourably to using SL in their learning remains to be seen (Kirriemuir, 2007). The recent Joint Information Systems Committee (2007) survey showed that students had low interest.

The social tools

It is the social nature of Library 2.0 which may prove to be the most important. Public libraries in the USA and Canada have grasped this in a multitude of instances (Block, 2007), for instance by staking their claim in MySpace (e.g. Contra Costa County Library, www.myspace.com/ourlibrary), Facebook, developing instant messaging, blogs, and the use of LibraryThing. Michelle McLean's chapter documented the early stages of this development, but we can expect it to snowball as services assess their impact on popularity and usage.

Although libraries need to get social, the extent to which we should push our efforts in this direction has drawn a variety of responses. Brooklyn College (www.myspace.com/brooklyncollegelibrary) was a trendsetter in establishing a MySpace account, to be where the users are. It may be, however, that students do not want us in 'their' spaces, and will migrate elsewhere. Dawn Lawson of New York University set up a Facebook account to communicate with students but had a 17% response from 140 messages (8 Friend requests and 5 reference questions; Lawson, 2007). However, contact through these networks may yet provide the facility to reach out to those who may not have contacted us otherwise, and offer one-to-one support.

As Facebook has opened up its API to developers, users can now add their chosen applications to their Facebook profiles. This has opened up new possibilities. The ability to use a widget on Facebook to link to a library catalogue is powerful, as Facebook becomes like a home page for some students. Some libraries will be able to get their IL message across more easily by suggesting that their students link to subject guides which could be accessible through Facebook. This would be possible if the library uses the open source Springshare LibGuides software, and the student then adds the LibGuides application to their Facebook profile.

The use of these applications should be seen as an extra opportunity to reach students, and we must remember that we would need to keep renewing these solutions if Facebook were replaced by some other social networking wonder (Cohen, 2007).

Schools, further education and to some extent higher education are facing difficulties in establishing policies for access to social networking sites. Libraries inevitably get involved in these turf wars, and more often defend the right to access websites, dislike censorship and are reluctant to draw distinctions about what can be considered 'academic use'. The number of machines may be inadequate to meet all demands and this can cause the blocking of what appears to be recreational use. We can expect this conflict to continue if education and libraries embrace the social networking sites that students use to communicate with one another. The same conflict could occur with the academic use of gaming. Librarians who use active learning methods are likely to employ exercises and games. As these become more sophisticated they may be delivered on the web. Illinois Mathematics and Science Academy (IMSA) internet search challenges is one such example (http://21cif.imsa.edu/tutorials/challenge).

The new sharing

The ability of Web 2.0 services to function as databases of content should be considered. Tim O'Reilly, in a recent keynote speech at the Graphing Social Patterns Conference, said that Web 2.0 was really about 'systems that harness the network effect to get better the more people who use them', which implies building collective databases (Ammirati, 2007).

The use of del.icio.us as an alternative to Google for finding material should also be considered. The ability to harness the collective tags of others as opposed to search engine metrics adds a new dimension to search. Del.icio.us is therefore a powerful tool for allowing collaborative research (Thompson, 2007). Although it relies on tagging by individuals, the ability to choose tags already used by others helps to create what is called a 'folksonomy'. As Bryan Alexander said, 'finding people with related interests can magnify one's work by learning from others and leading to new collaborations', and tagging 'can offer new perspectives on one's research, as clusters of tags reveal patterns (or absences) not immediately visible' (2006, 36). This means that librarians will be recommending del.icio.us to their users for storage of their bookmarks and for sharing with others in a class. Blackboard, the major higher education VLE in the UK, released Scholar in 2007, which is a mix of bookmarking with some elements of a social networking site. Its reception has been mixed (Leaver, 2007) because of its limitation in enabling sharing only within the Blackboard community, which can be seen as a strength or a weakness. I suspect there is no danger of its replacing either del.icio.us or Facebook.

Jan Radford, a school librarian at Delany College, Australia, also uses del.icio.us for quick posting of recommended material (Rethlefsen, 2007). Public libraries will use tag clouds as ways of connecting with their users in a way that traditional subject indexes have been unable to do, because of their currency, visibility, snappiness and flexibility.

Technorati and Google Blog Search are already significant sources enabling us to search the blogosphere. Flickr is a valuable collection of visual material which can be used to support our teaching by using Creative Commons material. YouTube and perhaps the developing TeacherTube contain useful teaching material. SlideShare is the most well-known service for sharing presentations (www.slideshare.net).

Flickr can act as a repository for library photos of events and developments, which is easily accessible, and can be used for both promotion and IL teaching. As we have seen in Cameron Hoffman and Sarah Polkinghorne's chapter, tagging in Flickr is a powerful means to create understanding about keywords and controlled vocabularies. There has been research which shows that tagging helps users to create meaning. MacGregor and McCulloch (2006) and Golder and Huberman (2006) felt that tags helped users to create meaning, especially from sharing tags, and in their survey of data from del.icio.us in June 2005 concluded that stable patterns of tagging, despite minority variation, did occur.

The path toward Web 3.0

Libraries are no longer primarily about search. As Stephen Abram has observed, 'no-one comes to the libraries to search. Users come to us for learning, community, and other services' (Albanese, 2006). In the era where content is king, the use of faceted taxonomies and the advent of tagging and folksonomies are provoking considerable interest. Faceted systems can be traced back to library classification, whereas the philosophy behind tagging is threatening to upset many previous notions of the invincibility of the existing taxonomies used in libraries. David Weinberger, in particular, has written of the three orders of information (Weinberger, 2005): in the first we arranged books on a shelf, in the second we built up catalogues with metadata separately from the books allowing access from several different points of view, and now in the third both the data (books, journals, etc.) and the metadata have gone digital. This means that everything has changed: items have a distinct identification (URL), but do not have to be described as part of a structured list (taxonomy) or even have a definitive shape, because their essence will become clearer through descriptors derived from user tagging. As we have seen, these collections of tags have grown into folksonomies, and their power for resource discovery is only just being experienced, through Web 2.0 tools like del.icio.us, LibraryThing and Flickr. Investigation into their use within library OPACs is progressing, for example with the WPopac at Plymouth State University Lamson Library, an adaptation of an Innovative Interfaces OPAC (Furner, 2007). The more descriptors used in these services, the richer the mixture will become. At the same time, the development of the Resource Descriptor Framework (RDF) aims to provide a standard way to describe the most important relationships of a topic in a particular area of knowledge, by what has become known as 'triples' (the format subject/predicate/object). The resulting ontologies could provide immensely detailed metadata in these specific areas of knowledge into ontologies that could be used together to move toward what has been called the Semantic Web.

As we move toward Web 3.0, Web 3D, or the Semantic Web, what will this imply for information control? These developments will result in objects on the web no longer just being anonymous hyperlinks but having well defined attributes which can be understood by machines. Another way of expressing this is 'an evolving extension of the world wide web in which web content can be expressed not only in natural language, but also in a format that can be read and used by software agents, thus permitting them to find, share and integrate information more easily' (http://en. wikipedia.org/wiki/Semantic_web).

A glimpse of what this could look like can be gained from such sites as Freebase (www.freebase.com/signin/), a shared open database of the world's knowledge, and JeromeDL (www.jeromedl.org/), a digital library built on semantic technologies, which combines user tagging with ontologies (Kruk, 2007). This implies that in future the user will have the potential to discover a much richer flavoured collection of material, as the information which is searched will be uncoupled and recoupled according to the changing flow of knowledge.

Information overload has been, and will be, overcome by the way we have generated more information about information (Weinberger, 2007): that is to say both metadata and the linking capabilities available on the web. Hyperlinking in Wikipedia, and library services employing user tagging, are significant in that they represent the 'new' browsing, which for so many years researchers have been complaining was missing from digital sources. Will the combination of ontologies, and metadata in databases, combined with user tagging and the use of hyperlinks, at last provide both the precision searching and the browse facility so beloved of researchers?

Mobile technology

We can predict that mobile technology will be developing in spectacular ways over the coming months. Tomi Ahonen at Mobile 2.0 in San Francisco in October 2007 (MacManus, 2007) was hailing the mobile as 'the first personal mass media'; always switched on, carried around, and having creative potential. The launch of the iPhone across the world will attract great user attention and may thus act as a useful driver for new developments. Librarians will be exploring the potential for communication, promotion, text responses and catalogue access via mobile technology. Mobiles may be able to act as camcorders, and WiFi networks may facilitate affordable videocasting (Kelly, 2007). We may be moving toward a blended environment where material can be accessed from several platforms. More threatening is the practice of disposable applications in a climate of changing fashion in hardware.

Final thoughts on IL and Library 2.0

Tom Friedman believes that certain attributes will be really significant for employees in the flat world (Friedman, 2006): intellectual curiosity, passion about the job, and the ability to create the personal touch. Stephen Abram (2007) has also said that we should teach about success and knowledge management. I believe that IL can contribute to all of these. Elmborg (2003) also said IL 'can be a vibrant and interesting subject if it emphasizes the process of searching and researching' as we encourage the thrill of the chase. I believe our efforts will be made more powerful and meaningful through the use of active learning techniques in the Web 2.0 environment.

In the world of information scarcity, publishers mediated the content which was published and added to the world's knowledge. At first the web simply continued this process. Although at that time individual expression was possible on the web it was technical and difficult. Web 2.0 changed all this and in the age of the amateur, we are beginning to see the development of new forms of authority. In the days before Wikipedia we were taught to accept the text of Britannica as gospel: users of Wikipedia can now turn to edits, history, discussions about the article, and at the same time begin to realize that Britannica may not be right every time just because it was written by 'experts' (Weinberger, 2007). Newer forms of ranking include Google page ranking, which is good for finding answers, but not for gathering intelligence; Flickr and YouTube have developed a type of 'voted on by tag'; Slashdot remixes and comments on material by spotting trends; social networking sites rely on numbers of friends and comments; and Technorati's method of determining blog authority. In a Web

3.0 world we can expect the development of computer-assisted methods to filter quality. The National Academies Press Search Builder and Reference Finder may point the way toward tools which can pull out key phrases algorithmically (Jensen, 2007). The digital environment may provide the possibility of calculating all kinds of measures of authority which are impossible at present (e.g. percentage of a document quoted in other documents; raw links to the document; significance of author's other works). In a 3.0 world, the electronic text will be available for quoting, categorizing and tagging. Jensen believes that the present system of authority may continue in academia for another ten to 15 years, but I suggest that other measures of authority will be arriving on the scene soon: controversial and yet another trend which IL librarians will need to watch.

Technology has enabled the cut-and-paste generation to ignore the niceties of intellectual property. The significance of this element of IL will continue to grow, as a responsibility of schools, FE and HE institutions to educate their clientele. This understanding of ethical use can cover everything from students re-using material in onscreen video and making presentations to outside groups using copyrighted materials, to putting compromising material on Facebook and plagiarizing digital material. These issues go beyond the librarian into institutional policy, but we can assist by creating understanding of intellectual property.

The IL models may remain similar, and phenomenographic studies are illuminating how IL is perceived and will continue to illuminate how it should be taught. Opposition to 2.0 often comes in the guise of 'we have been doing all this before': rather like the opposition of staff toward IL as a term, as opposed to user education. We must acknowledge that Web 2.0 technologies are disruptive because of their instability, liability to change with fashion and the lack of support available. There is a danger that the process will never settle down: it is in its nature to move in fits and starts. The process will therefore be complex and we need not fear to experiment. We should utilize the tools, not for their own sake, but only where they improve our services, for the benefit of our users. This is likely to mean we will involve users: even Janet Fletcher, a stern critic of much of IL teaching, admits the importance of this in our future (Fletcher, 2006). The crux of the matter is this: how long should libraries spend gauging the success of the Web 2.0 pioneers' experiments? Or do they just jump in and roll out their own versions? As the technology is freely available, with plenty of opportunities to be creative, offering new ways to reach some of our users in a way that should appeal to them, the chance should not be missed. It is a matter of staffing levels, enthusiasm and state of mind. This book should help you to make that decision.

The importance of the information-literate person being able to interpret the context of what is found, based on healthy scepticism of everything they see on the web of the future, is critical. As understanding of this is experienced, learning occurs. In other words, we help students to construct meaning from what they find (Jastram, 2006). What has changed is that they will be doing this more often in a collaborative, active way because of the use of Web 2.0 tools. IL, the most important of the patchwork of capabilities which will help them make sense of their world, has undoubtedly been greatly enriched by the availability of these new participatory tools.

References

Abram, S. (2007) Next Two Weeks, *Stephen's Lighthouse* (blog), http://stephenslighthouse.sirsidynix.com/archives/2007/09/next_two_weeks.html.

Albanese, A. R. (2006) Google is Not the Net, *Library Journal*, www.libraryjournal.com/article/CA6370224.html.

Alexander, B. (2006) Web 2.0: a new wave of innovation for teaching and learning?, *Educause Review*, **41** (2), 32–44, www.educause.edu/apps/er/erm06/erm0621.asp.

Ammirati, S. (2007) Tim O'Reilly: Graphing Social Patterns Conference Keynote, *Read/WriteWeb* (blog), www.readwriteweb.com/archives/tim_oreilly_graphing_social_patterns.php.

Barnes, K., Marateo, R. C. and Ferris, P. (2007) Teaching and Learning with the Net Generation, *Innovate*, **3** (4), http://innovateonline.info/index.php?view=article&id=382&action=synopsis.

Bivings Group (2007) *American Newspapers and the Internet: threat or opportunity?*, www.bivingsreport.com/2007/american-newspapers-and-the-internet-threat-or-opportunity.

Block, M. (2007) Library 2.0 Means Better Service. Presentation given at British Columbia Library Association, 19 April, http://marylaine.com/lib20.html.

Bradley, P. (2007) *Facing the Challenge of Web 2.0 as a Disruptive Technology*, Internet Librarian International 2007, www.internet-librarian.com/Presentations.

Carnegie Mellon University (2007) Podcasting: a teaching with technology white paper,
http://connect.educause.edu/blog/jklittle/podcastingateachingw/44653.

Catone, J. (2007) Web 2.0 Backpack: web apps for students, *Read/WriteWeb* (blog), www.readwriteweb.com/archives/web_20_backpack_web_ apps_for_students.php.

Cohen, L. B. (2007) 2.0: a failed promise without transparency, *Library 2.0 an Academic's Perspective* (blog),
http://liblogs.albany.edu/library20/2007/08/20_a_failed_promise.html.

Deschamps, R. (2007) We Asked for Web 2.0 Libraries and We Got 2.0 Librarians, *The Other Librarian* (blog),
http://otherlibrarian.wordpress.com/2007/08/15/we-asked-for-20-libraries-and-we-got-20-librarians.

Elmborg, J. K. (2003) Information Literacy and Writing Across the Curriculum: sharing the vision, *Reference Services Review*, **31** (1), 68–80.

Fletcher, J. (2006) *Information Literacy is Dead?*,
www.information-online.com.au/docs/Presentations/information_literacy_ is_dead_final_paper.pdf.

Friedman, T. L. (2006) *The World is Flat: the globalized world in the twenty-first century*, Penguin.

Furner, J. (2007) *User Tagging of Library Resources: toward a framework for system evaluation*, www.ifla.org/IV/ifla73/papers/157-Furner-en.pdf.

Golder, S. A. and Huberman, B. A. (2006) Usage Patterns of Collaborative Tagging Systems, *Journal of Information Science*, **32** (2), 198–208.

Gorman, M. (2007) Web 2.0: the sleep of reason, part II, *Britannica Blog*
http://blogs.britannica.com/blog/main/2007/06/web-20-the-sleep-of-reason-part-ii.

Grassian, E. and Truman, R. B. (2007) Stumbling, Bumbling, Teleporting and Flying . . . Librarian Avatars in Second Life, *Reference Services Review*, **35** (1), 84–9.

Greenhill, K. (2007) 10 Ways to Find Time for 23 Things, *Librarians Matter* (blog), http://librariansmatter.com/blog/2007/09/03/ 10-ways-to-find-time-for-23-things.

Guhlin, M. (2007) Why Teachers Use Web 2.0, *Around the Corner* (blog), www.edsupport.cc/mguhlin/archives/2007/09/entry_3594.htm.

Houghton-John, S. (2007a) Future of Libraries Conference: social software in the library – MySpace, wikis, IM, blogs, and Flickr, *LibrarianInBlack* (blog), http://librarianinblack.typepad.com/librarianinblack/2007/09/index.html.

Houghton-John, S. (2007b) We'll Come to You, *LibrarianInBlack* (blog), http://librarianinblack.typepad.com/librarianinblack/2007/09/well-come-to-yo.html.

Jastram, I. (2006) Information Literacy 2.0, *Pegasus Librarian* (blog), http://pegasuslibrarian.blogspot.com/2006/10/information-literacy-20.html.

Jensen, M. (2007) The New Metrics of Scholarly Authority, *The Chronicle of Higher Education,* http://chronicle.com/free/v53/i41/41b00601.htm.

Joint Information Systems Committee (2007) *Student Expectations Study,* www.jisc.ac.uk/media/documents/publications/studentexpectations.pdf.

Keen, A. (2007) *The Cult of the Amateur: how today's internet is killing our culture and assaulting our economy,* Nicholas Brearley.

Kelly, B. (2007) The Future as Today, But More So, *UK Web Focus* (blog), http://ukwebfocus.wordpress.com/2007/09/20/the-future-as-today-but-more-so.

Kirriemuir, J. (2007) An Update of the July 2007 'snapshot' of UK Higher and Further Education developments in Second Life, Eduserv Foundation, www.eduserv.org.uk/upload/foundation/sl/uksnapshot092007/final.pdf.

Kruk, S. R. (2007) *Digital Libraries of the Future,* www.slideshare.net/skruk/digital-libraries-of-the-future-use-of-semantic-web-and-social-bookmarking-to-support-elearning-in-digital-libraries.

Lawson, D. (2007) *Using Social Software to Reach Library Patrons,* www.internet-librarian.com/Presentations.

Leaver, T. (2007) *Scholar: Blackboard's (anti)social bookmarking platform/extension,* http://tama.edublogs.org/2007/01.

Lippincott, J. K. (2006) *Net Gen Learners and Libraries,* www.lib.umd.edu/groups/infocommons/NETGENLearnersLippincott.pdf.

MacGregor, G. and McCulloch, E. (2006) Collaborative Tagging as a Knowledge Organisation and Resource Discovery Tool, *Library Review,* **55** (5), 291–300.

MacManus, R. (2007) Mobile 2.0 – the 7th mass media and business opportunities, *Read/WriteWeb,* (blog), www.readwriteweb.com/archives/mobile_20_7th_mass_media_business_opportunities.php.

McIntyre, D. (2007) A Free Online Wall Street Journal? *Bloggingstocks* (blog), www.bloggingstocks.com/2007/09/19/a-free-wall-street-jounal-online.

Nino, T. (2007) Second Life and the Future of Web 2.0, *Second Life Insider*, (blog), www.secondlifeinsider.com/2006/11/15/second-life-and-the-future-of-web2-0.

O'Connell, J. (2007) Digital kids – learning their own way, *HeyJude* (blog), http://heyjude.wordpress.com/2007/10/12/digital-kids-learning-their-own-way.

Rethlefsen, M. L. (2007) Tags Help Make Libraries del.icio.us, *Library Journal*, www.libraryjournal.com/article/CA6476403.html.

Sanger, L. (2007) *Why the Citizendium will (probably) succeed*, www.citizendium.org/whyczwillsucceed.html.

Secker, J. (2007) *Social Software, Libraries and Distance Learners: literature review*, http://clt.lse.ac.uk/Projects/LASSIE_lit_review_draft.pdf.

Thompson, J. (2007) Is Education 1.0 Ready for Web 2.0 Students?, *Innovate*, **3** (4).

Weinberger, D. (2005) Trees and Tags: an introduction, *Journal of the Hyperlinked Organization*, www.hyperorg.com/backissues/joho-mar03-05.html.

Weinberger, D. (2007) *Everything is Miscellaneous: the power of the new digital disorder*, Times Books.

WILU (2007) It's All Fun and Games Until Someone Loses an Avatar, *WILU* (blog), http://wilu.wordpress.com/2007/05/24/its-all-fun-and-games-until-someone-loses-an-avatar-library-instruction-in-a-3d-virtual-world-a-second-life-collaborative-project.

Index